Counseling *the* *Hard Cases*

A Critical Review

Martin and Deidre Bobgan

Scripture quotations are taken from the
Authorized King James Version of the Bible

Chapter 5, The Appendix, and some other portions of this book have been adapted from former writings by Martin and Deidre Bobgan.

"Counseling the Hard Cases"
A Critical Review

Copyright © 2016 Martin and Deidre Bobgan
Published by EastGate Publishers
4137 Primavera Road
Santa Barbara, CA 93110

Library of Congress Control Number 2015918650
ISBN 978-0941717-24-3

Printed in the United States of America

Thus saith the LORD, Stand ye in the ways, and see, and ask for the old paths, where is the good way, and walk therein, and ye shall find rest for your souls.

Jeremiah 6:16

Study to show thyself approved unto God, a workman that needeth not to be ashamed, rightly dividing the word of truth. But shun profane and vain babblings: for they will increase unto more ungodliness.

2 Timothy 2:15-16

Table of Contents

1

A Critical Review

Biblical counseling has been growing in status within the evangelical community along with the increasing use and popularity of psychological counseling, which took hold shortly after the middle of the twentieth century. Since some Christians wanted biblical help rather than worldly psychological help; a biblical look-alike was created. Although the intent was to replace psychological counseling, which is based on a psychological understanding of man, with a biblical ministry based on biblical truth regarding the nature of man, much of what we call the biblical counseling movement (BCM) reflects psychological theories and therapies. In many cases what biblical counselors do is simply not biblical!

The errors of the movement show forth in what might be considered the stellar example of the best of what the BCM has to offer: *Counseling the Hard Cases* (*CTHC*), co-edited by Stuart Scott and Heath Lambert. Rightly stating the superiority of what God says and does over what psychology has to offer, Scott and Lambert, both seminary professors in biblical counseling, say in their "Concluding Reflections":

> The editors and contributors all believe that the Bible is comprehensively sufficient to deal with any problem that requires counseling. Additionally, we believe that both the descriptions and prescriptions of human problems found in God's Word are far superior to anything that secular psychology has to offer. Only God understands the problems of humanity at the deepest level—and how to fix them.[1]

While we are in agreement with this statement and have taught similarly for many years, **we are in drastic disagreement with how their aspirations are carried out in most of the ten cases presented in *CTHC*.**

Before launching into this critique of *CTHC*, some disclosure on our part is necessary. Importantly, we believe and have taught for over 40 years that the Word of God and the work of the Holy Spirit in the fellowship of the saints are sufficient to deal with the nonorganic issues of life without sending Christians out of the church to psychotherapists. Additionally those who suffer from the biological trials and tribulations of life can profit greatly from biblical ministry as they seek help. We have taught and practiced from the beginning that **all the personal, relational issues of life which are now popularly referred to licensed psychological counselors for "cure" through conversation can best be done through those in the church ministering to one another**. Building up the church spiritually is far more important than erecting biblical counseling offices, which in many ways are often just knock-offs of what psychological counselors do.

Scott and Lambert subtitle their book *True Stories Illustrating the Sufficiency of God's Resources in Scripture*. While on the one hand we believe, practice, and teach the "Sufficiency of God's Resources in Scripture" for the "hard cases" of life, we demonstrate in this critical review that the hard cases presented in the book are not "True Stories." The ten cases are all reconstructions or remembered cases from the past and **lack the literal dialog of the original biblical counseling sessions to qualify as "True Stories."** They are at best approximations of "True Stories," which likely contain some of the natural, fleshly, inadvertent twisting of actuality, which would happen to all who attempt to restore the reality of an original case. **Anything less than a literal live case with literal live dialog is less than the literal live truth.** The less it is of the literal live case, the less accurate it is likely to be. Look at all the Bible verses used, look at all the educational and professional credentials of the counselors, look at all the happy endings to the cases. Note also the slick, seamless counseling stories that are told, **but do not believe any of the *CTHC* cases to be true stories, because they are not truly true**.

Problem-Centeredness

One of the key reasons we left the BCM years ago is its problem-centeredness, which often involves sinful talk about problems in a manner similar to those in the psychological counseling movement.[2] **In fact, biblical counseling as conducted today is nowhere found in Scripture**. According to David Powlison, a leader in the BCM, biblical counseling as conducted in the BCM is newly arrived in the church.[3] Although biblical counseling was designed to help people with the Bible rather than with psychology, the *CTHC* hard cases reflect the psychological counseling movement in many of its methods, practices, and procedures, which are very problem centered.[4] Those who say they are being biblical often practice the same sinful problem-centeredness that inevitably leads to sinful speaking about self, situations, and sufferings.[5] Biblical counselors such as those in *CTHC*, much like their psychological counterparts, place a high degree of emphasis on determining the root cause of problems through observing external behavior or by looking for "idols of the heart."[6]

In checking all the instances of counseling in the Bible, there is no example of a woman or of a man being counseled about the kinds of personal problems often discussed in biblical counseling. No instances occur in the Bible with individuals or couples murmuring or talebearing in a biblical counseling type of setting. Because the ten cases in *CTHC* are not live cases in that the full dialog of the conversations is not given, much of the murmuring and talebearing that normally occur in biblical counseling are not revealed. Also there is neither one-to-one cross-gender nor marital counseling anywhere in the Bible. Thus, the terms used and the problem-centered conversations are from secular counseling and should be avoided by all who desire to be truly biblical in ministering to others. **There is no biblical precedence or examples of any of this! Those who function in this way, plus other ways mentioned later, are merely following those in the psychological counseling movement. In fact, if the psychological counseling movement did not exist, the biblical counseling movement would not have followed in its footsteps in the problem centered-**

ness in which it currently exists, and that certainly applies to the ten recreated cases in *Counseling the Hard Cases.*

Counselor, Counselee, Counseling

In speaking about the biblical counseling movement (BCM), we use the terms *counselor, counselee,* **and** *counseling* **because that is their terminology.** The three words *counselor, counselee,* and *counseling* are the three most popular words to describe who does the counseling, who receives the counseling, and the type of conversation between them. **The way these terms are used in the BCM and in** *CTHC* **does not match the use of these words in Scripture. Moreover, not one of these roles (counselor, counselee) or activity (counseling) of the modern biblical counseling era equates with anything in Scripture.** (See Appendix)

It is understandable that those in the BCM and those counselors who did the ten "hard cases" in *CTHC* use the contemporary terms *counselor, counselee,* and *counseling,* because these three worldly words rightly fit what they do, since their counseling is reflective of the psychological counseling movement. As a matter of fact, the ten "hard cases" use the words *counselee(s)* (83 times), *counselor(s)* (100 times), and *counseling* (73 times) for a total of 256 times. In contrast, we use the word *minister* for what we believe Christians should do to help fellow believers in need. The word *minister,* along with its variations, is found over 200 times in the Bible. If one checks the various Hebrew and Greek words translated *minister* and its variations, it should be obvious that *min-*

ister is the right biblical word and activity to use among believers rather than *counseling*.

Most of the words in the New Testament that are translated *minister(s), minister(ed), ministering*, and *ministry* come from words that have to do with serving, helping, and supplying what is needed as from a position of servant rather than from a position of one exercising dominion and authority over others. In other words, all who **minister according to the Bible** do so at the foot of the cross, dependent upon the work of the Holy Spirit, and under the authority of the Lord and His Word. While the biblical word *ministry* and its variations are used in *CTHC*, the unbiblical use of the terms *counselor, counselee*, and *counseling* predominates.

We found it odd that in all of *CTHC*, out of 143 "counsel" verses in the Bible, only Proverbs 20:5 is quoted, but not to justify the kind of counseling that biblical counselors do. Perhaps they assume that what they do is biblical and requires no justification. A word of caution: Christians are used to and frequently use the words *counselor counselee*, and *counseling*. We do not personally correct individuals or couples who use those words when they come to us for help. However, when we describe the help we provide, we refer to it as *ministry* rather than as *counseling*.

CTHC **Counselors**

The backgrounds of the contributors to *CTHC* emphasize the credence those in the BCM give to educational backgrounds. The contributors to *CTHC* are two MDs, two PhDs, one PsyDs, four DMins, and one RN. While on the one hand we would not rule out such backgrounds, on the other hand we have, in our training and calling others to mutual care ministry, ignored educational credentials and emphasized the importance of finding believers who: (1) are knowledgeable in the Word, (2) are filled and gifted by the Holy Spirit to minister to others, (3) have shown through their behavior that they are growing in sanctification, (4) and have walked with the Lord and been dependent upon Him through their trials in life. Such knowledge, life, gifts, and callings become apparent as believers come to know one another in the Body of Christ in the local church.

The *CTHC* counselors are a somewhat limited, one-sided, in-house group in that seven of the ten counselors belong to the Biblical Counseling Coalition. Though they come together from different origins and backgrounds, they all share the same BCM mentality. Also, it is noteworthy that, of the ten counselors, only two are women, even though at least two-thirds of the counselees are typically women. Nevertheless, that is understandable since the men in the BCM believe it is their biblical prerogative to counsel women, and, yes, even alone! Whenever we have asked them, "Did you ask the husband's or father's approval to counsel his wife or daughter?" as the case may be, they answer "no," wondering why we would even ask. If this one wholly unbiblical practice of men counseling women, especially without the husband's or father's approval, stopped, that would be a dramatic change for the BCM.

Most of the counselors contributing to *CTHC* spend far too much time attempting to analyze the flesh, "the old man, which is corrupt according to deceitful lusts" (Eph. 4:22). In doing so, they succumb, some naïvely, to recycling psychological interpretations and reframing them into biblical terms. While they may sound erudite, they are wasting their time analyzing the flesh, because even if one aspect is identified and corrected, it will only be replaced by another. The heart of the old nature will always be deceitful (Jer. 17:9). Although it may be re-framed and reformed, it is still the flesh, "the old man, which is corrupt according to deceitful lusts." When they are in this mode, they are attempting to help their clients understand their flesh, rather than to count it dead (useless, putrid, sinful, and rotting). What many biblical counselors do best at times is teach the Word, clarify biblical doctrine, and guide people into putting off the flesh, being renewed in the mind, and putting on the New Life, which is Jesus living in them through the blessed Holy Spirit. In contrast, so many of these writers are analyzing the past and the heart of the old nature and attempting to identify "idols of the heart."

Lack of Internal Criticism

There seems to be an unspoken agreement that biblical counselors are not to be critical of sinful practices within the movement. Because internal criticism happens so infrequently, it is a sure sign of how weak the biblical counseling movement truly is. We challenge leaders in the biblical counseling movement to openly criticize unbiblical practices and teachings of leaders in the movement, document those errors, and **provide the names of leading biblical counselors and/or popular organizations that are in biblical error.**

The only popular review naming names of teachers is by Lambert in his PhD dissertation-turned-book. Specifically he names and critiques Jay Adams, the first person to whom he dedicates the book. However, Lambert makes himself clear when he says:

> This is a book about how biblical counselors have grown up and matured since the initial leadership of Jay Adams, but it is not a strike against Adams. To the contrary, the ministry of Jay Adams changed my life, and I love him. One of the great honors of my life has been to get to know him a bit over the last several years.... Beyond any personal connection, I believe Adams has been one of the most consequential men in church history in the last 150 years. His work revolutionized the way thousands of people do ministry. In the last forty years everyone who ministers the Scriptures or has had the Scriptures ministered to them according to the principles of biblical counseling has Jay Adams to thank.[7]

Lambert does say that "Jay Adams' work was imperfect"[8] and he once criticizes him for "an unbiblical harshness" in a talk. No person in Lambert's book is exposed for being unbiblical, even his fellow seminary professor Eric Johnson, who deserves the label.

It is strange that there is such a reluctance to name names of those in the biblical counseling movement who are involved in unbiblical practices when Adams, who fathered the modern-day, newly arrived movement, wrote the following in his endorsement for our book *PsychoHeresy: The Psychological Seduction of Christianity*, defending us for doing so:

> Some people will say the Bobgans are hitting too hard—naming names and all that—but I don't

think so. Whenever someone writes for the Christian public he sets forth his views to the scrutiny of others, but if others think what he says is dangerous to the church they, like Paul (who named names too), have an obligation to say so.[9]

Adams has also said elsewhere:

> Any Christian who sets himself up as a teacher in the church of Christ and publicly teaches anything thereby opens himself up for criticism by others (cf. James 3:1). If they think what he is teaching is harmful to the church, they have an obligation to point it out just as widely as it was taught. Such public warning or debate on a topic should not be considered a personal attack at all.... What a critic of a public teaching does in pointing out his disagreement with that teaching has nothing to do with personal affronts or lack of reconciliation; he is simply disagreeing at the same public level as that on which the teaching was given in the first place.[10]

This same standard should be applied to anyone who criticizes any individual or organization in the biblical counseling movement.

Scott and Lambert's "Preface"

In their rush to beef up their bragging rights about counseling the "Hard Cases," Scott and Lambert say, early on, that counselees from the 10 cases "sought help from secular, medical, and religious professionals before finally coming to biblical counselors for help" (p. xi). This impression is repeated in some of the cases and serves to dramatize by contrast the success of the ten cases that follow and the inferred success of others in the BCM. Such remarks accentuate the seeming past failure of professionals' and others' attempts to help and thus elevate the status of biblical counselors. This is a not-too-subtle boastful contrast to puff up and promote the ten cases that follow, as well as biblical counseling in general. Surely Scott and Lambert must know that, after "they sought help from secular, medical, and religious professionals," some? many? have **come to biblical counselors, received counseling, and been worse off!**

The editors refer in the "Preface" to the disagreements and "differences of opinion" that exist regarding the "sufficiency of God's Word to administer an effective counseling ministry." They speak about being "united by something much more profound—the blood of Jesus Christ." They proceed to say:

> In light of that union, it is regrettable when the exchanges between our various groups are not loving and productive. We want to confess plainly in this book that you are our brothers and sisters in Christ, and we love you (p. xii).

This comment and throughout *CTHC* is proof positive that those in the biblical counseling movement (BCM) wish to remain harmoniously irenic at the cost of failing to expose the error that is running rampant among them and the integrationists as well as the Christian psychotherapists. They are ironically irenic, but, while all the leaders of the BCM that we know claim a heritage from the Reformation, they cannot name one Reformation leader who was irenic in his disputations. In fact, if any of the leaders of the Reformation were living today they would be biblically blunt, blatant, and prominently public about their concerns of what goes on in the name of the Bible among many of those in the BCM. The editors of *CTHC* have a biblical responsibility for naming names of individuals and organizations even though that may not seem "loving and productive." They have a greater obligation to expose by naming names those who are in error, which is the most loving thing that can be done for the most people involved and that especially includes criticizing leaders in the BCM.

Speaking to a vast audience who will read *CTHC* and saying that "you are our brothers and sisters in Christ," when there are many who might read this book whom Scott and Lambert would clearly not know well enough to declare that they are saved (brothers and sisters in Christ), sounds like sheer flattery. Many of us know individuals who have talked the talk, been in church for years, and even seemingly been born again, who were not saved, but some of whom later come into the faith. Hopefully we can all agree that only God truly knows who assuredly belongs to Him. We can call believers with whom we are spiritually acquainted "brothers" and "sisters," but to identify a vast unknown audience in that manner is frankly an unbiblical assumption. In addition, to say to this vast unknown audience, "we love you," without critically naming names as did Jesus and the apostle Paul, sounds more gratuitous than biblical. Moreover, Scott and Lambert are implying that those who disagree with them are "not loving and productive" while they themselves are "loving and productive" even to the point of saying, "we love you." God's people are admonished to love family, neighbors, and even enemies. Jesus and the apostle Paul spoke repeatedly of love. However, Jesus critically confronted the Pharisees and others and Paul even "delivered unto Satan" both Hymenaeous and Alexander (1 Tim. 1:20), but Jesus and Paul never coupled their criticisms with a baseless bouquet of "I-love-you's."

Scott and Lambert's Lynchpin

As we reveal later, the lynchpin for Scott and Lambert's house of cards is their view of mental illness. Their fallacious view is a disaster in the making and a danger to those who counsel and their counselees. Believing, teaching, and promoting such a view of mental illness will lead to calamities as it places in litigious danger those who will foolishly follow and copy-cat counsel with confidence accordingly. This can easily be a great detriment and disaster to those who receive such counseling.[11]

Be aware and very wary of Scott and Lambert's view of mental illness, as it is not only a functional backdrop to the ten cases in *CTHC* but also sets an example for all those in the BCM to follow. *CTHC* is sure to be read by a vast majority of biblical counselors because it is written by ten of the BCM leaders. Because of this, we write with utmost concern and anxious alarm over the possible compounding consequences of those in the BCM mimicking Scott and Lambert in their unproven notion.

Additional reasons why we recommend against believing and following the practices exemplified in the ten cases are related to general unbiblical practices of those in the BCM. Reading our entire critique will save both those who counsel and those who are counseled from unbelievable, unbiblical practices and potentially dangerous ideas being carried out.

WARNING: Do not blithely, blindly and blatantly play follow-the-leader with the ten case studies showcased in *CTHC*. Do not take literally these ten cases and the inferred claim that you, too, can cure[12] through biblical counseling the hard cases listed in *CTHC* plus, by extension, the other 300 mental disorders[13] listed in the *Diagnostic and Statistical Manual of Mental Disorders* (*DSM*) that do not have medical markers and where no organic issues are found after a full medical workup!

Schizophrenia?

In Chapter 1, titled "Introduction: The Sufficiency of Scripture, the Biblical Counseling Movement, and the Purpose of This Book," Heath Lambert's main theme is the sufficiency of Scripture for the hard cases. Lambert quotes Ed Welch as saying that the Bible is "able to speak to the common problems we all encounter.... But it also speaks to **distinctly modern problems** such as depression, anxiety, mania, **schizophrenia** and attention deficit disorder, just to name a few" (p. 17, bold added). Welch is in error in that the problems listed are not "distinctly modern problems," but merely modern names for symptoms that have always existed. However, Welch's theme about the use of the Bible is coterminous with Lambert's sum and substance subject of the sufficiency of Scripture for the "Hard Cases." Lambert notes that students ask about such hard cases as "**schizophrenia**, sexual abuse, eating disorders, bipolar" and "dissociative identity disorder" (p. 24, bold added). The only other place **schizophrenia** is mentioned in *CTHC* is on page 172 where it is said, "The people who accept our invitation often come with difficult issues to overcome: **schizophrenia**, bipolar disorder, suicidal to name a few" (bold added). However, that chapter is about "'Tony and Bipolar Disorder." Schizophrenia is listed in passing as one of the hard cases. Nevertheless, there is **no example** in all ten *CTHC* cases of schizophrenia being cured, let alone dealt with. But, a cursory reading of *CTHC* would lead one to conclude that schizophrenia can also be dealt with through Scripture alone, along with the other "Hard Cases." With no clarification by Scott or Lambert as editors, such statements are extremely egregious.

Schizophrenia is one of the most enigmatic of the mental disorders and its **cure** has been elusive to this day. **For Scott and Lambert to casually set aside the billions-plus dollars spent and the multitudinous hours labored on research on schizophrenia by brilliant minds in their effort to promote their personal opinion about a scriptural cure for schizophrenia is reprehensible!**

Harvard Medical School reports: "One in a hundred persons will at some time suffer from schizophrenia. **Its causes are obscure, and no way is known to prevent or cure it**" (bold added).[14] In his book *Surviving Schizophrenia*, E. Fuller Torrey, MD, refers to schizophrenia as "today's most misunderstood illness" and says:

> Contrary to the popular stereotype, schizophrenia is an eminently treatable disease. That is not to say it is a curable disease, and the two should not be confused. Successful treatment means the control of symptoms, whereas cure means

the permanent removal of their causes. Curing schizophrenia will not become possible until we understand its causes; in the meantime we must continue improving its treatment.[15]

Torrey further says, "Psychiatric disorders can be caused by genetic, infectious, metabolic, and other organic etiologies, some of which are detectable by a physical exam and blood tests, but **many cannot be**."[16] Psychiatrist Laura Hendrickson, MD, the biblical counselor who does the first case in *CTHC*, says, "There is no known cure for schizophrenia."[17] In contrast, Scott and Lambert's view of a biblically curable schizophrenia is held by many biblical counselors and will be held by many more and pursued by others who undiscerningly read *CTHC*. This is doubly bogus by those who practice according to this view, first by the fact that true schizophrenia has no known cure, and, second, because Scott and Lambert list it as a spiritual disorder curable by biblical means. That is not to say we cannot minister Christ to schizophrenics as we have in the past and currently do.

Where's the Warning?

As we said, *CTHC* deals with the "hard cases," which they list as "schizophrenia, sexual abuse, eating disorders, bipolar," and "dissociative identity disorder." The book communicates to those who have such labeled disorders and to others that the Bible is sufficient to deal with such mental disorders as long as they are not "organic malfunctions affecting the brain" (p. 8) and are "nonmedical problems." The chapters of *CTHC* describe dealing with these disorders in such a way as to give hope by presenting a biblical counseling alternative to those readers who have been diagnosed with one or more of these mental disorders and may be taking or considering taking psychotropic medications.[18] *CTHC* could lead them to question or change the use of them. **Unfortunately the necessary and usual responsible warning about psychotropic medications is entirely absent at the beginning, which is a major mistake of this book**, may put some readers at risk, and may leave the authors and publishers open to a potential lawsuit. **When describing cases regarding ordinary problems of living for which people seek counseling, such a warning is not necessary.** However, when describing "hard cases" and specifically naming the hard cases that are covered in *CTHC* and listed in the *DSM*, **a warning is a dire necessity**. This warning should be placed somewhere on the front pages, even if it has to be pasted on the current, already printed copies.

Dr. Peter R. Breggin, who is probably the best-known psychiatrist in America for his opposition to psychotropic medications, has a full-page warning at the beginning of his best-known book, *Toxic Psychiatry*.[19] His very first words, emphasized by italics, are: "*Do not abruptly stop most psychiatric drugs!*"[20] Note the exclamation mark! Dr. Laura Hendrickson, a psychiatrist and a "diplomate, American Board of Psychiatry and Neurology,"[21] is the author of the first case of *CTHC*. We have previously critiqued her writing and speaking.[22] In her coauthored book *Will Medicine Stop the Pain?* Hendrickson says she was "diagnosed bipolar disorder" and was on psychotropic medication. She describes herself as having had "suicidal thoughts," but after having met with her pastor she experienced rapid recovery and says, "In fact, it was the medicine that went off the bridge instead of me."[23] In spite of this veiled possibility for others to do likewise, Hendrickson does give "A Word of Caution," which is totally lacking at the beginning of *CTHC*. Although we have ministered to many hard cases over the years, we have never written about such cases to demonstrate that the Bible can indeed be used in such circumstances. However, if we did, knowing that some of those who would read what we write would either be on psychotropic medications or consider using them, we would certainly issue a warning as did Breggin and Hendrickson.

The *DSM*, the psychiatric bible for mental illnesses, has over 300 mental maladies in its latest edition (*DSM-5*).[24] As we shall reveal later, the *CTHC* biblical counselor can counsel most all of them **by the standard set forth in *CTHC***. Considering a possible number of 300 different mental disorders for biblical counselors to tackle and the fact that psychotropic drugs are available for nearly all of them, one would expect the authors of *CTHC* to be especially careful to sound the warning that is normally given.

However, there is no early warning, and that needs to be corrected, because it is a serious omission, a great disservice to the readers, and could have serious consequences for the counselees. They do not have a "warning" introductory page as Breggin did in his book and "A Word of Caution" as done by Hendrickson in her coauthored book. One exception to this omission is in Dr. Dan Wickert's case in which he rightly and nicely expresses caution to the reader, but such a caution should be at the beginning rather than later (pp. 120 and 121), since readers might not reach that page before they toss their medi-cations "off the bridge," as Hendrickson did, especially if they identify with an earlier case in the book. Because of this lack of warning next to the implied promises of what biblical counselors can do with the hard cases, *CTHC* **is a potentially litigious bomb that may be exploded on biblical counselors who naively follow the lead of the ten cases**.

2

Cases, Anecdotes and Science

Scott and Lambert, co-editors of *Counseling the Hard Cases (CTHC)*, each have a chapter discussing a "hard case." John MacArthur wrote the Foreword and the book includes endorsements by David Powlison, Lance Quinn, Deepak Reju, and Wayne Mack. We question the subtitle of their book, *True Stories Illustrating the Sufficiency of God's Resources in Scripture*, because the *CTHC* stories lack the complete accuracy of true stories. While it is not like the five blind men and the elephant each describing the elephant from his own limited point of view, it does smack of the counselor seeing the counselee and the counseling from the counselor's own biased and sinful heart (Jer. 17:9) picking and choosing, interpreting, and understanding what is seen, heard, experienced, and reproduced as a case. [1] The old adage, "We see things not as they are but as we are" applies in such situations. What is left out may be as important or more important than what is included. Literal dialog of each of these ten cases would surely expose the fleshly sanitized versions that appear in *CTHC*.

Case Studies

We will now discuss the use of case studies and why we object to their use.[2] Scott and Lambert say that some cases have the "details of the problem" while "other case studies are composites" that are the result of "blending the stories of several different counselees." And, "Some contributors have obtained explicit permission from those they helped to share their stories without anonymity" (p. xiii). All ten of the counselees are presented in quotes around their names, meaning that these are not their real names, and frankly these are not their real stories in spite of what is said, as we will explain.

Regardless of which of the ten cases are composites and which are claimed to be real stories, none contain the full, exact dialogs that would be the result of live sessions and therefore **all are reconstructions**. We repeat, instead of being real stories, these are reduced redacted reconstructions of real stories. In other words, these cases are not literal accounts. It is **not** necessarily what the biblical counselors say, as many are quite erudite in their writings; it is **not** necessarily what they claim to do, with which we are often harmonious; it is **not** just their refined reconstructed cases, which any literate counselor can create; **it is what they do through literal live dialog that is a testimony to how unbiblical they can be**.[3]

Case studies are often used in psychological and biblical counseling to show forth the usefulness of a particular idea or methodology. Aside from using brief examples to illustrate a point, we are opposed to the use of case studies for a variety of reasons. Drs. Elizabeth Loftus and Melvin Guyer wrote a two-part article with the subtitle "The Hazards of the Single Case History." They began by saying:

> Case histories have a long and cherished tradition in science. They are compelling anecdotes, often powerful enough to generate entire theories of behavior. Freud built the edifice of psychoanalytic theory on the very few cases he saw in therapy. Bruno Bettelheim used a few cases of autistic children to conclude that autism is caused by "refrigerator" mothers. Psychiatrist Cornelia Wilbur's account of her patient, "Sybil," captivated millions of people who believed the story of Sybil's "multiple personalities."[4]

All of these theories, based on "very few cases," have been powerfully influential in the practice of psychotherapists; but **all have been debunked**. Loftus and Guyer say:

> But case studies, by definition, are bounded by the perceptions and interpretations of the storyteller. If they are well told . . . readers often find them far more persuasive and compelling than the stodgy numbers and cautions of science.[5]

Dr. Paul Meehl, a past president of the American Psychological Association, once wrote an extensive paper as to "Why I Do Not Attend Case Conferences," in which he indicates a multitude of reasons for his concerns. The case conferences of which Meehl is speaking are meetings in which a single case or a number of cases are discussed by the individuals present. However, some of his concerns and complaints apply equally well to *CTHC* with both its cases and comments by the editors. Meehl, a practicing psychotherapist, says, "The main reason I rarely show up at case conferences is easily stated: the intellectual level is so low that I find them boring, sometimes even offensive." Meehl contrasts the counseling psychology case studies with that of internal medicine and neurology about which he says, "both of which I have usually found stimulating and illuminating."[6]

Because Meehl's paper is 85 pages long, we will just quote from a few of his complaints. He first refers to a "Buddy-buddy syndrome" and adds:

> In one respect the clinical case conference is no different from other group phenomena such as committee meetings, in that many intelligent, educated, sane, rational persons seem to undergo a kind of intellectual deterioration when they gather around a table in one room.[7]

While on the one hand *CTHC* authors are not in a committee meeting, they are all in the biblical counseling family and recognize each other as players on the same team cooperating in each of the ten cases to prove the *CTHC* point. Meehl's next complaint is that "All evidence is equally good." He refers to a "mush-headed approach which says that everybody in the room has something to contribute." In such a setting, the cases and the authors in *CTHC* have a common respect and common goal to show the world that biblical counselors can indeed counsel cases no matter how hard they are; the camaraderie and commitment to a common goal with no criticism concludes in what Meehl would say is a "mush-headed approach." Meehl's next complaint states, "Reward everything—gold and garbage alike" where "Nobody gives anybody negative reinforcement."[8] All ten cases are positively presented with positive results to push the common agenda seemingly at all costs. Meehl says, "A corollary of the 'reward everything' policy with respect to evidence and arguments is a substantive absurdity, namely, everyone is right—or at least, nobody is wrong."[9] The very idea that "nobody is wrong" permeates the bottom line for the ten cases, because, if there is one wrong, it might just suggest that *CTHC* is a house of cards ready to fall. Meehl goes on adding one complaint after another.

Scott and Lambert say that *CTHC* is "a book of stories" and that each case is an individual situation. They say of each case:

> It is not a methodology that describes how you should proceed with every counselee experiencing a similar problem. Of course there will be commonalities and overlap, but it is essential to affirm that in God's world no two situations are exactly the same. Though the chapters provide methodological guidance for how you might move forward in comparable situations, please do not assume that what is appropriate in one context is always appropriate in another (p. xiv).

This is a very mixed message! The editors say, "no two situations are exactly the same" and "do not assume that what is appropriate in one context is always appropriate in another." They also say, "there will be commonalities and overlap" and "the chapters provide methodological guidance for how you might move forward in comparable situations." This is very contradictory. If truly "no two situations are exactly the same," that should bring into question the usefulness of any commonalities and methodologies provided. And, what are comparable situations? **This is one more reason why the 10 cases should be taken with a grain of salt.**

While brief examples may be all right, one should not be intimidated by the biblical counseling cases in *CTHC* that appear to prove an approach or point of view of the biblical counselor or to demonstrate how to be a successful counselor even with the 300 possible disorders in the *Diagnostic and Statistical Manual of Mental Disorders* (*DSM*). (See Chapter 3.) It is time for Christians to give up trying to learn how to counsel by studying or listening to anecdotes and cases. In addition to other reasons given above, anecdotes and case studies can get in the way. Two people could have exactly the same external problem, but only God knows the complexity of the specifics of what and how for a particular person. That is why we say that those who minister to one another need to get **in** the way but **out** of the way. They need to be available, but they need to let God work rather than push their own agenda or employ methods and techniques championed by some self-styled human biblical counseling "expert."

These cautions apply to all counseling cases. If we were presenting a case, it would be easy enough to put words in the mouth of our fictional counselor and create composite responses as done in *CTHC* on the part of the counselees with their counselor. Anyone who has counseled for a period of time could contrive a composite case to prove the value of whatever is done. Each one could take a very different approach from the leading biblical counselors and present a composite case with equally difficult challenges and a happy ending. All who claim to be biblical counselors, no matter how different from or how contradictory to one another, could contrive a composite case to "prove" whatever they wish, especially if they are gifted story tellers. **The variety of biblical counseling approaches should be judged not on the number of Bible verses used, but rather on whether or not they are truly being biblical in practice.**

As one reads the case studies in *CTHC*, one may become impressed with how erudite and facile the counselors appear to be in analyzing others, but don't automatically believe it. One does not need to be erudite or facile and one should not be analyzing others. Instead, one needs to be biblical, not analytical. In fact, the more erudite and facile sounding one is in analyzing, the less truly biblical one is likely to be. In addition, as often happens in counselor-reported cases, a number of self-congratulatory remarks are included, which we note along the way.

In our reading of psychological counseling case studies over many years, we see a greater honesty with respect to some discussion of cases and their positively reported outcomes than in *CTHC*. Psychotherapists as well as biblical counselors are not generally critical of one another. However, psychotherapists, unlike biblical counselors, do have critical case commentaries, such as in *Psychotherapy Networker* and in other professional journals and books. [10]

We could enumerate with many examples. The following was revealed by a psychotherapist in a professional journal regarding what happens after therapy sessions:

> But then they go home, and far more often than we'd like, when they're back in their daily lives

> with family, friends, and coworkers, they don't do so well. In fact, no matter what progress they make *in* therapy, once they leave the safe, rarified space we provide them in our treatment rooms, they frequently fall right back into the same old patterns of negative emotion and dysfunctional relationships (emphasis hers)....
>
> Most clinicians believe that the benefits of individual therapy should naturally transfer to the rest of a client's life. But what if that's not necessarily true? What if the positive interactions a person has with a therapist in the "inside" world of the consulting room don't translate into the language of relationships conducted in the "outside" world of the person's everyday life?[11]

However, like most counselors describing their work, the psychotherapist does go on to compliment herself.

The following is another of many excellent examples of the sort of self examination of the practice of psychotherapy by two psychotherapists. These two psychotherapists speak of "a curious set of rules" that exist in counseling and say, "the rules are quite different from the rules for ordinary relationships. The most striking difference is that the **usual expectation of reciprocity disappears**" (bold added).[12] All the drama and narrative dialogue are about the counselee and her issues and problems. The counselee gets to talk about herself and her litany of personal problems and the counselor does not get to talk about herself and her litany of personal problems, except for something brief that might be said to establish rapport. The expectation is that the focus of the counseling will be on the counselee's "problems and life and words."[13]

The two authors describe how normal friends will seem mundane after a therapeutic love-in that can occur in counseling. They aptly describe such skewed relationships:

> The special partnership that allows a therapist to earn a good living and a patient to focus on neglected aspects of his life and experience would be a disaster outside of the office. Used as a template for other intimate relationships, it is selfish and self-absorbed. Other than therapists, only an occasional very self-sacrificing parent or a spouse who aspires to martyrdom is likely to sign on for that long term. A problem with psychotherapy is that it can make all other relationships look like they fall short when it comes to sustained, attentive caring and leave the patient circling back to therapy as the only relationship that is good enough.[14]

If one replaces the word "therapist' with "biblical counselor" and "psychotherapy" with "biblical counseling," the application would be the same. No such confessions are made in the biblical counseling movement (BCM) as biblical counselors avoid critiquing and become dovish when doing so. And, never have we found that sort of honesty and transparency among biblical counselors! As for discussion of cases that totally failed, some exist in the psychological counseling movement, while none exist that we have found in the biblical counseling movement. One of the many reasons we left the biblical counseling movement is because there is little or no authentic self-examination in the movement. The closest in the ten cases are with Kevin Carson and Robert D. Jones. While we compliment two of the cases for some transparency more than the others and although parts of other cases come close, we are opposed to the promiscuously public presentation of all such case studies as they are another piggy-backing on and a replication of the psychological counseling movement. A rhetorical question to consider is: **If the psychological counseling movement with its case histories had not existed, would there be any biblical counseling case histories, considering that none existed before the rise of either movement?**

Those of us who minister to others can ignore any failed cases that we all have and take any success story and reconstruct it to our own making, especially combining "details of...different situations" (Heath Lambert) and "composites from other cases" (Robert D. Jones). The truth will always be revealed by a literal dialog of actual live sessions and will never be an accurate case if only done by reconstruction. Even great successes that we all have as we minister over a period of time have set backs in individual sessions that are only exposed through literal live counseling dialog.

Anecdotes

One huge difference between psychological counseling and biblical counseling is the fact that psychological counseling is subject to researchers researching their claims. No such activity or accountability takes place with biblical counselors. The anecdotal cases and claims by psychological counselors are subjected to statistical examination, but no such examination is done to the anecdotal cases and claims of biblical counselors. We summarize research conclusions of psychological counseling in "Ingredients for Successful Counseling" from *PsychoHeresy* (Revised & Expanded):

> In summary, the **counselee** is the keystone to successful counseling. This fact is the reason for psychotherapies being about equally effective (equal outcomes phenomenon), with the exception of those that produce as much as a 40 percent harm…. **In other words, the counselees who are motivated to succeed, who engage in the rapport with the counselor (therapeutic alliance), and who believe that they are receiving a valid treatment (placebo effect) will most likely succeed, regardless of the counseling approach and regardless of the counselor being an amateur or professional.** Therefore, counselees who meet these conditions and are given entirely different types and even contradictory therapies tend to have similar mild to moderate success rates.[15]

These same ingredients apply to successes in biblical counseling, though there is little admission to such possibilities by those in the BCM and especially not recognized in the ten *CTHC* cases.

Biblical counseling cases and claims rest solely on the anecdotal say-so's of the counselors. The ten case studies in *CTHC* are personal anecdotes written by the ten counselors. They are personal testimonials as to what happened during the counseling sessions and how successful the results. However, testimonials and anecdotes absent scientific proof should not necessarily be believed for psychological or biblical counseling.

We know of many extreme examples based on anecdotal claims with cases presented, in which the writers believe that all mental-emotional problems absent any known organic cause should be dealt with solely through biblical counseling. One of the more bizarre is in the book *Breakdowns are good for you*! The subtitle is *A unique manual for True Biblical Counseling*.[16] The cover asks a provocative question, which reveals the authors' approach. They ask, "Is self-pity the cause of 'mental illness'?" The authors are Rev. Dr. Robert J. K. Law and Malcolm Bowden. Both of these men, who are very astute theologically speaking, explain in their book why the answer to the above question is "yes."

Law and Bowden declare: "**All problems that can be dealt with and solved in counseling sessions are always due to the pride, self-centeredness and self-pity of the counselee**" (bold theirs).[17] They also say, "It is when people cannot get their own way and feel hard-done-by that they can descend into self-pity and begin to display one or more of the many forms of 'mental illness.'" They declare: "Get rid of self-pity and the 'mental illness' will disappear."[18] A one-sentence summary of their position is: "the fundamental cause of all" mood disorders is the "self-pitying and sinful response of people to difficult situations."[19]

A most bizarre example of biblical counseling is found with Pastor Henry Wright in his book *A More Excellent Way*, in which he teaches the so-called spiritual roots of diseases and claims that if someone is not healed there is a spiritual root that needs to be dealt with. He reports a plethora of cases anecdotally and numerous testimonials about an extensive list of disorders. Wright claims that women develop breast cancer because of "the sins of conflict and bitterness between the female and either her mother and/or her sisters or mother-in-law,"[20] and, "Lupus is rooted in extreme self-hatred, self-conflict, and includes guilt."[21]

We give these two examples to dramatize the need for understanding that we are dealing with anecdotes for all the biblical counseling we have critiqued and that includes the ten cases in *CTHC*. While we have in the past and still do minister to those individuals who would be labeled by Scott and Lambert as "hard cases," we have chosen to ignore the hard case labels and minister to the individuals as fellow believers before the cross of Christ. We see no need to compete with those who have arbitrarily developed the labels as in the *DSM-5* or those who therapize such labeled individuals. We minister to those individuals who have personal and spiritual needs and ignore their secularly driven labels and those practices that therapize them. We also see no need to plummet into the past history of individuals or plunge into the "idols of the heart" as described and practiced by so many biblical counselors.

BCM's Science Failings

We share in common with those in the BCM that psychological theories and therapies are not science but we depart from them in that we regularly quote what the scientific research has to say about various psychotherapeutic claims for its **effectiveness**. While the psychological theories and therapies are not science, nonetheless the scientific method (meta-analysis, etc.) can be used to evaluate their success claims. **This avoidance of the results of scientific research on psychological counseling and its implications for biblical counselors is one of the great failings of the BCM**. While it is true that research employs scientific methods, it does not follow that whatever is being investigated is scientific. Many non-scientific and even questionable practices, such as E.S.P., biorhythms, fingertip reading, and psychic phenomena, have been investigated by scientific research procedures. The scientific method has been used to investigate everything from art to Zen and from prayer to politics. We certainly would not call all of these "science."

The senior editor of a professional psychotherapy journal says:

> Therapists by and large don't really like science, don't believe it's particularly relevant to their work, and in fact, often seem to regard research and therapy as antagonistic entities—as if you can be a good therapist *or* a good scientist, but not both.[22] (Emphasis in original.)

Replace "therapists," "therapy," and "therapist" with "biblical counselors," "biblical counseling," and "biblical counselor" and the resulting statement would be true. This admitted dichotomy between researchers and practitioners exists even more among biblical counselors.

David Murray, a leader in the BCM, in a moment of criticizing the movement, says:

> When compared with biblical counselors, [Ken] Ham and his creationist colleagues seem to be much more informed about the science they are

interacting with and much more capable and courageous in entering the scientists' world, taking the scientists' facts and findings, and re-framing them within the biblical worldview.

I don't see so much evidence of that in biblical counseling, a field I read a lot in, teach in, and do almost daily as well. What is much more common is disinterest in, hostility towards, or even outright rejection of the whole field of psychology and pharmacology IN PRACTICE. Note these last two words. I don't doubt the "we embrace the same facts" theory, as Heath Lambert ably articulates it. But where's that actually being practiced and who is actually practicing it?[23]

Lambert was shocked by Murray's criticism and, in his attempt to contradict it, lists a psychiatrist, a number of medical doctors, and others with advanced degrees of various kinds in his attempt to prove otherwise.[24] Instead of producing various individuals and their educational backgrounds to contradict the no-research-science accusation, Lambert needs to produce evidence in answers to the questions we raise throughout this review. In the psychotherapeutic world there are two groups of individuals: one group is that of the practitioners (psychotherapists); the other group is that of the researchers who bring reality and restraint over any run-away claims of the practitioners. In our various writings we provide endnotes to research on psychological counseling that we believe applies to biblical counseling, but we have never seen such noted by those in the BCM.

The BCM is relatively free of the researchers peeking or poking into what they do in their cloistered counseling offices. Thus they are free to make claims unimpeded by a need to prove anything. To our knowledge there has rarely been scientific research establishing the **effectiveness** of the various forms of biblical counseling. There are probably as many forms of biblical counseling as there are biblical counselors, even though their hierarchical organizations expect their followers to follow the formulated formats and methodologies of the leaders.

We have never seen references in the BCM writings to the negative research findings of psychological counseling that probably exist with biblical counselors, but never reported by them. For example, never have we seen raised the question of possible harm that may be caused by biblical counselors. A summary in the *Handbook of Psychotherapy and Behavior Change* reveals: "Readers will note that the topic of negative effects arises in various chapters in this book, and researchers seem to have no doubt that deterioration or negative outcomes can and do occur."[25] We have never seen such research quoted and related to the possible harm rate of biblical counseling.

Regardless of the counseling approach (psychological or biblical), the two most important factors for success mentioned earlier are the personal qualities and circumstances of the one who comes for help and the rapport that exists between the counselor and counselee. **The current research stresses the great importance of rapport for success in counseling and calls it the "therapeutic alliance."** This term and its significance in successful counseling is repeatedly seen in the literature.[26]

A *Psychology Today* article says:

Researchers who compare the success rates of various schools find that by and large, techniques and methods don't matter. What does matter is the powerful bond between therapist and patient. The strength of this "therapeutic alliance" seems to spell the difference between successful therapy and a washout.[27]

The *Harvard Mental Health Letter* refers to the therapeutic alliance and says that it is "the working relationship between patient and therapist that is probably the most important influence on the outcome of therapy."[28]

Psychotherapy Networker says:

> The incontrovertible evidence is in: studies of the top 25 percent of therapists—those whose success rates are at least 50 percent better than the average—show unequivocally that neither training, experience, personality style, theoretical orientation, nor (get this) innate talent—has anything much to do with what makes the greats better than all the rest…. The therapeutic alliance—the ability to engage a client in therapy, to forge and maintain a strong, personal connection with her, convince her that the two of you are on a common path—remains the single most important element of all therapy.[29]

John C. Norcross and Marvin R. Goldfield, in their academic text of psychotherapy research and results, estimate that the counselee and the rapport (therapeutic alliance) if established by the counselor would average about 70 percent of the success with **counselee or client factors being the greater of the two**.[30]

Dr. Arthur Shapiro, clinical professor of psychiatry at Mount Sinai School of Medicine, suggests that the power of psychological counseling may be the effect of a placebo. The placebo effect takes place when one has faith in a pill, a person, a process or procedure, and it is this faith that brings about the healing. The pill, person, process, or procedure may all be fake, but the result is real. Shapiro says:

> Just as bloodletting was perhaps the massive placebo technique of the past, so psychoanalysis—and its dozens of psychotherapy offshoots—is the most used placebo of our time.[31]

Dr. Hans Eysenck dramatically states:

> It is unfortunate for the well-being of psychology as a science that ... the great majority of psychologists, who after all are practicing clinicians, will pay no attention whatsoever to the negative outcome of all the studies carried on over the past thirty years but will continue to use methods which have by now not only failed to find evidence in support of their effectiveness, but for which there is now ample evidence that they are no better than placebo treatments.

He goes on to ask:

> Do we really have the right to impose a lengthy training on medical doctors and psychologists in order to enable them to practice a skill which has no practical relevance to the curing of neurotic disorders? Do we have the right to charge patients fees, or get the State to pay us for a treatment which is no better than a placebo?[32]

All of this and more add an exclamation mark to the question mark hanging over psychotherapy.

If psychotherapy indeed operates as a placebo, the psychological approach one uses does not matter. The patient will interpret what he is receiving as helping him whether it does or not. His thinking will then influence the result. We have never seen the placebo effect research referred to or even mentioned by those in the BCM as it might apply to biblical counseling.

In the research there are also other conclusions about psychological counseling that would be very beneficial for Christians to know, which we have never read or heard stated in biblical counseling circles, such as amateurs versus professional counselors. According to distinguished researcher Dr. Robyn Dawes, "the training, credentials, and experience of psychotherapists are irrelevant, or at least that is what all the evidence indicates."[33] Dawes also says that "the therapists' credentials—Ph.D., M.D., or no advanced degree—and experience were unrelated to the effectiveness of therapy."[34] It is amazing to us that Christians who have no psychological or biblical counseling training and may not ever have gone to college are so reluctant or may be fearful to minister to fellow believers when the research demonstrates the following:

> In a meta-analytic [research] review of studies that address level of training, Berman and Norton concluded that professionally trained therapists had no systematic advantage over nonprofessional therapists in evoking treatment gains.[35]

Dawes says:

> Evaluating the efficacy [effectiveness] of psycho-therapy has led us to conclude that professional psychologists are no better psychotherapists than anyone else with minimal training—sometimes those without any training at all; the profession-als are merely more expensive.[36]

This is not reported in the BCM literature with the implications for the BCM's emphasis on certification for counselors. Wouldn't it be beneficial for Christians who are without the counseling certificates or degrees of any kind to know this? Those in the BCM fail to refer to such scientific literature.

In our book *PsychoHeresy* we list numerous conclu-sions from psychological research about the effectiveness of psychotherapy, which may apply to biblical counsel-ing, but are never found in their literature. The effective-ness research from the field of psychotherapy would be valuable information for all biblical counselors to know, but it is absent from the BCM literature that we have read. **We conclude from reading a great deal of litera-ture on biblical counseling written by biblical coun-selors that either they are ignorant of the research on psychological counseling and its implications for biblical counselors or they do not care about it.**

3

"Organically Generated Difficulties"?

As we reveal in this chapter, Scott and Lambert's view of mental illness is the lynchpin for their house-of-cards theory about what constitutes "organically generated difficulties" in contrast to "nonmedical problems." The mental illness lynchpin is pulled by a scientific exposé of its fallacious foundation and correspondingly their house of cards, which is built around it, comes tumbling down. **The ten cases are predicated on no medical illness being found through a complete physical exam.** These ten cases serve as a model for other biblical counselors to read and follow after their counselees have had a complete medical exam that reveals no bodily illness related to the mental symptoms. The worst part of Scott and Lambert's fallen house-of-cards mental illness idea is what is communicated to all other biblical counselors, who will follow the lead because of the example established by ten highly educated, well-known, respected, and popular leaders of the biblical counseling movement (BCM). With two of the ten biblical counselors being medical doctors, one would think Scott and

Lambert would have been warned by them about such **an irresponsible conclusion**.

In Chapter 1 of *Counseling the Hard Cases* (*CTHC*) Heath Lambert favorable quotes Jay Adams, who says:

> Organic malfunctions affecting the brain that are caused by brain damage, tumors, gene inheritance, glandular or chemical disorders, validly may be termed mental illnesses. But at the same time a vast number of other human problems have been classified as mental illnesses for which there is no evidence that they have been engendered by disease or illness at all…. [The problem with the "mentally ill"] is autogenic; it is in themselves…. **Apart from any organically generated difficulties, the "mentally ill" are really people with unsolved personal problems.**[1] (First ellipsis and brackets Lambert's, second ellipsis and bold ours, p. 8.)

Later Lambert says: "**Biblical counselors believe that Christians possess everything necessary to help people with their nonmedical problems** (2 Pet 1:3-4)" (p. 13, bold added).

The statements by Adams and Lambert and similar ones by others imply that one can determine whether a person has "organically generated difficulties" or "nonmedical problems" and thereby lead many biblical counselors to conclude that all one needs to do is to recommend that a counselee have "a complete physical exam" (pp. 65, 97, 150, 177, 299). Referring the counselee to a physician is often one of the counselor's "first steps" (p. 214).

Serious errors result from this type of reasoning. **First is the mistaken idea that one can know whether or not mental symptoms that are not clearly "caused by brain damage, tumors, gene inheritance, glandular or chemical disorders" are actually "nonmedical problems."** One of the most difficult issues to deal with in counseling is the cause and treatment of mental disorders. There are numerous varieties of such disorders as the ones mentioned in *CTHC*: "schizophrenia, sexual abuse, eating disorders, bipolar" and "dissociative identity disorders," as well as depression. The big question is whether such "hard cases" are "organically generated difficulties" or "nonmedical problems." **The sum and substance of the *CTHC* assumption is as follows: Unless there are proven biological diseases that can account for the usual symptoms of mental disorders, the root causes and cures are spiritual and can be resolved biblically. Lambert says it succinctly elsewhere as follows: "Receiving a full medical work-up allows us to rule out organic issues."[2]**

Since we cannot always know whether or not there are "organically generated difficulties," one should not conclude, as is done in *CTHC*, that the mental disorders are spiritually driven, thereby only needing biblical remedies. We quickly add that those with life issues, whether "organically generated" or not, should be ministered to biblically as the occasion arises.

We referred to the *Diagnostic and Statistical Manual of Mental Disorders* (*DSM-5*) earlier and the need for a warning about psychotropic medications. Here we explain why the over 300 mental disorders listed in the

DSM-5 qualify for biblical counseling according to the standards set forth in *CTHC*. The main reason is that nearly all these mental disorders are based upon subjective reports by the clients because there are no obvious or clear organic, physical origins to support the diagnoses. The University of California *Berkeley Wellness Letter* reports:

> Mental illness is both extremely common—one in five Americans will experience a mental disorder in any given year—and extremely hard to diagnose in some cases, since no simple biological tests exist to detect them. There's no blood test for, say, depression or a personality disorder; no scan that can reveal attention-deficit hyperactivity disorder (ADHD). Instead, a clinician must rely solely on a patient's symptoms and observation of his or her behavior to reach a diagnosis.[3]

Dr. Jeffrey Lieberman, who is chairman of psychiatry at Columbia University and the current president of the American Psychiatric Association, says: "With rare exceptions such as narcolepsy, which can be diagnosed by testing cerebrospinal fluid, there are no objective biological measures for mental illness."[4] According to a major theme of *CTHC*, biblical counselors can counsel all but the "rare exceptions" because "there are no objective biological measures for mental illness." The *CTHC* belief is that, aside from these "rare exceptions," the *DSM-5* mental disorders are not, so far as currently known, "organically generated difficulties" and are therefore "nonmedical problems," which means they have spiritual roots and can be resolved biblically.

Scott and Lambert, as well as others in the BCM, are woefully naïve about the biological possibilities of the very "Hard Cases" they claim to cure. As we quoted earlier, E. Fuller Torrey, MD, a research psychiatrist says, "Psychiatric disorders can be caused by genetic, infectious, metabolic, and other organic etiologies, some of which are detectable by a physical exam and blood tests, but **many cannot be**" (bold added).[5]

Most competent practicing medical doctors who see patients regularly and any book written by a capable medical doctor on this subject will debunk this extremely erroneous idea and medical illness position of *CTHC*. For example, Erno Daniel, MD, PhD, an internal medicine doctor who has been at a large medical clinic for 30 years and seen patients on a regular basis, has written a book titled *Stealth Germs in Your Body*. In his chapter "What Else Could It Be?" he has a section titled "We Found Nothing" versus "There Is Nothing." Daniel says:

> Clearly there is a difference between "we found nothing (abnormal)" and "there is nothing (abnormal)." In general "we found nothing, so far" means that the screening examinations and tests that were ordered to look for particular conditions yielded negative results at the time they were done. In other words, nothing truly abnormal was found on the examination or on the tests that were chosen to be performed thus far. Clearly, that doesn't prove conclusively that you are not harboring stealth germs in your body, as there **is no foolproof test that can find everything. The absence of a large number of possible condi-**

> **tions does not exclude the presence of some other previously undetected or evolving condition** (bold added).[6]

Daniel later explains why exhaustive testing is not done in a section titled "Cost-benefit Considerations in Testing." He says:

> Most likely, you were only tested for conditions that were suspected to be causing your symptoms, and conditions for which there is specific effective treatment available. One of the main reasons why tests for many "nontreatable" conditions are not routinely ordered is because ethical doctors try not to incur unnecessary expenses. Although information obtained from some tests might be interesting, the tests usually won't be ordered if the results are not expected to yield direct benefit in correcting or managing your condition as demonstrated by evidence-based medical practices.[7]

Anyone reading the entire chapter of Daniel's book would see the reasons why one cannot rule out a medical condition when a complete physical finds nothing and **why Scott and Lambert's mental illness theme is a mental illness myth**.

The blunt truth is that no one, no matter how expert, educated, and experienced in the field of medicine, can say for sure about the hard cases where there are no medical markers whether or not there are "organically generated difficulties" involved or whether they are "nonmedical problems"! Thomas R. Insel, MD, director of the National Institute of Mental Health says:

> Mental disorders are among the most complex problems in medicine, with challenges at every level from neurons to neighborhoods. Yet, we know so little about mechanisms at each level. Too often, we have been guided more by religion than science. That is, so much of mental health care is based on faith and intuition, not science and evidence.[8]

Likewise, for Scott and Lambert, "so much of mental health care is based on faith and intuition, not science and evidence."

An article in *Psychology Today* reports that there are "100 billion neurons in the human brain" and that it would take 32 million years "to count each synapse in the human brain at a rate of one synapse per second."[9] An article in the *Psychotherapy Networker* describes the human brain as "the most complex biological entity known on earth." The author adds, "The number of possible interconnections among its neurons exceeds the estimated number of atoms in the universe."[10] The brain is obviously central to the mind-body relationship because it controls every organ system in the body. In addition, the brain also responds to every organ system within the body. This interaction of body to brain/mind and brain/mind to body is a complex process, and the enigma of it prevents us from knowing much truth about the underlying causes of mental symptoms. Knowledge is limited because the secrets of human behavior are locked up in the brain-mind-body relationship and particularly in the brain.

Michael Chase, in an article entitled "The Matriculating Brain," wrote, "The human brain, for all our intimacy with it, has surrendered less to scientific research than have the distant moon, stars and ocean floor, or such intimate processes as genetic coding, immune reactions or muscle contraction."[11]

We begin with the axiom that humans have a brain/body (biological) and a mind (nonphysical). The intimate relationship between the brain/body and the mind has led to misunderstanding and misdiagnosis during the entire history of psychiatry and psychotherapy. The problem of biological disorders that were thought to be psychological problems and treated as such is a grim skeleton in the therapeutic closet. Most psychiatrists and psychotherapists would like to ignore or forget about this history of looking at and treating psychological symptoms that were really the result of physical diseases not identified at the time.

At one time in this history there were undetected physical diseases that were treated as mental disorders because of the accompanying mental symptoms, and that is still true today. Two examples are general paresis, caused by the spirochete of syphilis invading the brain, and pellagrous psychosis, caused by a dietary deficiency of nicotinic acid. In both cases multitudes of people who have suffered from these diseases were labeled schizophrenic and treated accordingly.

This raises the whole problem of misdiagnosis and the tendency to refer people to psychotherapists or psychiatrists. And, it opens the door for biblical counselors to assume that no "organically generated difficulties" or medical problems exist when none are found and therefore the person has a spiritual problem in need of biblical answers. There have been and still are great numbers of individuals wrongly referred to psychotherapists or psychiatrists who are really suffering from physical disorders. Also there are a number, we know not how great, who are counseled by biblical counselors because bodily disorders have not been found.

Sydney Walker III, a neuropsychiatrist, says:

> Each year, hundreds of thousands of Americans who are actually suffering from common medical conditions such as hyperthyroidism, Lyme disease, and even poor nutrition are misdiagnosed with psychiatric disorders. Studies show that the rate of misdiagnosis is more than 4 in 10.[12]

In the *Scientific American Mind*, an article titled "Ruled by the Mind" says, "Many common ailments and physical conditions can influence the brain, leaving you depressed, anxious or slow-witted." The article discusses some somatopsychic disorders in which "the root of the problem [mental disorder] lies in the body—and in particular the immune system."[13] There are many bodily disorders that doctors do not relate to the mental symptoms that result from them. An article in the *Wall Street Journal* titled "Confusing Medical Ailments With Mental Illness" refers to "more than 100 medical disorders" that "can masquerade as psychological conditions or contribute to them, complicating treatment decisions." The article states, "Recognizing an underlying medical condition can be particularly difficult when there is also a psychological explanation for a patient's dark moods."[14] **Think about the possible prolific personal harm that can result from assuming a spiritual cause and biblical cure for the 300 mental disorders**

listed in the *DSM* as can often happen with the "Hard Cases" counseled by biblical counselors!

There is a whole range of bodily disorders that have mental symptoms. Some of these biological disorders are in their embryonic stages—not yet detectable. These symptoms can result in mental disorders that would be diagnosed by biblical counselors as spiritual problems requiring biblical solutions. There is a whole class of diseases called "idiopathic." According to the dictionary, "Idiopathic is an adjective used primarily in medicine meaning *arising spontaneously* or *from an obscure or unknown cause*."[15] In other words, there are **no biological markers** for such diseases; there are **only symptoms**. There are many such diseases of the body and brain that occur, and we assume that biblical counselors would have to agree that there are idiopathic diseases of the body that are known only by their symptoms. If logic prevails, biblical counselors would have to say, "**No discernible biological, bodily markers means no biological, bodily problems**." Just as diagnosing idiopathic **bodily** diseases that lack biological markers must rely upon symptoms, diagnosing idiopathic brain diseases that lack biological markers must also rely upon symptoms.

What about true bodily or brain disorders or **diseases yet to be discovered**, whose symptoms are mental, emotional, or behavioral? As we just noted, there are all sorts of mental disorders that have been treated in the past by psychiatrists as psychological disorders that later were found to have physical causes. Because "organically generated difficulties" were not found at the time, those disorders would have been diagnosed as psychological by psychologists, but spiritual by biblical counselors, needlessly and foolishly foisting unneeded counseling on unsuspecting counselees.

Just as there may be **no biological markers** that clearly reveal the etiology of various mental disorders there are also **no spiritual markers** for them. In regard to **spiritual markers**, all of them are symptomatic, e.g., church membership, personal testimony, words, actions, financial giving, teaching, Christian family, Bible college or seminary degree, being a pastor, etc., none of which can be said to be a certain sign that one is a believer. It is as serious an error to assume that those with mental disorders without biological markers are suffering exclusively for spiritual reasons as it is to assume that those with mental disorders without biological markers are suffering exclusively for biological reasons. **How sad it is when a Christian diagnoses a fellow believer's mental disorder as spiritually caused when, indeed, there may be hidden biological reasons for the symptoms.** To be fair-minded one needs to avoid categorically placing individuals who are without biological markers into either a spiritual or a medical box because only God knows the nature and extent of each. Beyond the obvious cases, such as brain tumors, etc., **the ones who are biologically afflicted but do not have biological markers are known only by God**. Only God knows for sure when biological markers are absent whether there is a spiritual or biological cause and whether a spiritual or medical solution is all that is necessary.

In the absence of biological markers, spiritualizing a mental disorder and prescribing a biblical regimen alone can be a serious a mistake, because **counseling based on such wrong assumptions could induce guilt and**

greater suffering even for the most godly individuals, especially if there is no change in symptoms.. Wouldn't it be much better to admit that one may not know what underlies an individual's mental symptoms and yet provide spiritual helps that may alleviate the suffering and promote spiritual growth? Everything in life has spiritual overtones. However, every illness in life is not solely the result of our spiritual choices and that includes mental disorders, which can be the result of genetics, hormones, diseases, injuries, and circumstances, all of which can affect one's state of mind. And, of course one will respond to the issues of life biblically more and more as one grows in the spirit and matures in the faith. Therefore, one should seek to minister the things of the Spirit and build individuals up in the Word. Whether the problem is biological, spiritual, or both, believers may minister God's mercy, grace, and truth to fellow believers, because **every occasion of suffering can be used for comfort and spiritual growth—unless the one who ministers thinks he can diagnose another person's heart attitude.** There must be much humility in personally ministering to those who are suffering, even if they have brought this suffering upon themselves.

Let's say a woman who is suffering from a mental disorder is not a believer. Let's say by the mercy and grace of God she is converted, but her mental disorder remains. In such cases, **some** may be delivered from mental disorders. However, others, because of biological impairment not yet discovered, will continue to suffer as long as the body/brain is affected. Yet, during that time a believer who continues in depression may draw close to the Lord and find comfort and encouragement in time of need.

While the authors of *CTHC* may wonderfully bring forth the use of Scripture, they woefully leave their readers in danger of suffering from mental symptoms believing that their current spiritual life is causing these distressing symptoms and is responsible for their current state of mind and that, as soon as they "straighten out" spiritually, their mental disorder will be over. **This will surely cause many such believers to feel guilty about their own "spiritual lack" when they may be as spiritually sound as the authors of *CTHC* themselves. *CTHC* is a great discredit to those godly individuals and a great disservice to the church.**

Often times only God knows if the mental disorder is caused in whole or in part by a spiritual problem, and therefore only God truly knows if a spiritual solution is all that is necessary. The biblical counselors' conclusion that a mental disorder is spiritual under the conditions they set encroaches upon God's territory. They need to repent of claiming to have knowledge that only God can truly know. It can be said that every mental and bodily disorder should include biblical ministry to the one who is suffering, but **not** to confront sin unless it is necessary and surely not to be fossicking around for idols of the heart.

Most practicing Christian medical doctors would not agree with the *CTHC* conclusion regarding medical testing that, if the testing is negative, there is no medical condition, but only a mental one that is actually a spiritual problem that one can diagnose and treat biblically. **There is no one on earth who can tell for sure whether a mental disorder that has no known biological mark-**

ers is a spiritual problem or a biological problem or a combination of the two!

Furthermore, brain imaging is still in its early stages of usefulness in diagnosing mental disorders. Certain problems, such as cell damage through tumors, strokes, and other mishaps, can be identified through brain imaging. But other activities in the brain having to do with neurotransmitters vary during the day and from day to day so that a specific diagnosis through brain imaging is definitely limited. Disease can be extensive, but not identifiable. Some diseases can be rampant and horrible but not even identified. **Therefore, it is worse than naïve to state definitively that mental problems that cannot be seen through existing medical tests, no matter how thorough, are spiritual problems.**

Let's take this no "organically generated difficulties" for the mental disorders to its logical conclusion. First we know that there are no medical markers for most of the hard cases. The hard cases that *CTHC* claims it can cure are "schizophrenia, sexual abuse, eating disorders, bipolar" and "dissociative identity disorders." **No medical markers that would be revealed through a most extensive medical examination would mean that everyone, without exception, who suffers from one or more of these conditions is merely suffering from spiritual problems of living rather than any biologically driven conditions!**

Logical Fallacy

We repeat, because mental disorders often have no biological markers to reveal their cause, Scott and Lambert conclude that both the cause and cure

of such disorders must be spiritual. We are concerned about the way biblical counselors are rigidly set in their spiritual/biological dichotomy, contending that mental illnesses are either the result of a **spiritual** problem or a **detectable** biological disorder. Biblical counselors are probably unaware of the fact that they are involved in an either/or logical fallacy. One logic book describes the either/or fallacy s follows:

> The *either/or* fallacy, sometimes called *false dichotomy*, consists of mistakenly assuming that there are only two possible solutions to some problem or that solving some problem consists of choosing between only two alternatives. The argument moves by showing that one of the alternatives is false or unacceptable and concludes that the other must be true.[16]

Based upon their naiveté about true diseases and their bogus either/or fallacy of true diseases and spiritual disorders, biblical counselors rush in "where angels fear to tread" to counsel individuals for whom no true bodily or brain disease has been found. **It may never have occurred to them that a mental disorder could be the result of a combination of a true disease and a spiritual disorder or a true disease not discovered during a complete medical examination.**

Mental symptoms can be related to a person's spiritual life, but to categorically say that it is either physical or it is spiritual is just plain wrong reasoning. There are many other bodily symptoms that consistency would demand that they be labeled spiritual disorders when no physical disease can be found. Backaches resulting in mental symptoms are frequent complaints that often escape a specific disease diagnosis to relate them to the brain. Are those backaches spiritual problems? Likewise for sinus and respiratory disorders that result in mental symptoms where no true disease is found to connect the two—are these spiritual problems? And how about the controversial disorders of fibromyalgia and chronic fatigue with doctors arguing on both sides of the body/mind issue. Also, how about headaches related to mental disorders where all the possible medical testing has been done, but the headaches persist? Since they affect the brain absent any biological markers, are these spiritual problems as well? What do biblical counselors do with the fact that women have "twice the risk of depression as men"[17] and two-thirds of those with General Anxiety Disorder are women?[18]

A recent article indicates that the "first blood test to diagnose major depression in adults has been developed."[19] Prior to this there was no such medical marker. Without knowing about this recent discovery and thus assuming the problem is spiritual, Scott and Lambert and other BCM counselors would assume the depression to be solely a spiritual problem if nothing is found in the usual "complete physical exam." Through the years the list of true diseases has expanded and will continue to expand as more cause and effect relationships are discovered. **Many disorders labeled "psychological" by the psychotherapists and "spiritual" by biblical counselors may be identified in the future as true diseases resulting in mental, emotional, or behavioral symptoms, thus bringing embarrassment to those who follow this foolishness.**

We repeat, in the past, when a reason for a symptom could not be found, psychiatrists jumped in with their psychiatric diagnoses. And, people were told that their symptoms were all in their head. In fact, there was a time when asthma was thought to be caused by family relationship problems. The biblical counselors have simply shifted the blame from the psychological to the spiritual, which for Christians becomes a hopeless cycle of condemnation and guilt on top of the symptoms already being experienced.

Some diseases creep in subtly, and some, which can cause mental symptoms in their early stages, are not identified for years. Because of the limitations of a physical exam, no matter how extensive, one may never know for sure if the mental symptoms have a physical base. Leaping to a conclusion that it is a spiritually related, as with an either-or fallacy (bodily or spiritual), after a complete physical that reveals nothing is naïve at best and cruel at worst when put into practice.

There are many examples we could provide from our own ministry experience and from other testimonies of overlooked physical causes of mental disorder symptoms. There are two cases of Christian women, with whom we are personally acquainted, who were diagnosed with psychiatric disorders because no known physical disease was discovered even after numerous physical tests and examinations by a variety of doctors. Both women were diagnosed as having a psychiatric disorder. In the first case, it was suggested that the woman's husband might possibly be involved in her disorder. After several years of struggling, she was finally found to be a victim of Lyme disease, which is caused by a deer tick. The second woman reported a number of psychiatric symptoms and was diagnosed with schizophrenia. Months later, after she had continued to suffer from the various symptoms, an astute doctor revealed that her symptoms were due to a viral pathogen. Can you imagine the damage the biblical counselors could cause with these two Christian women and many others?

During the period of time prior to the discovery of Lyme disease in the one and the virus in the other, with accompanying psychiatric symptoms in both, these two women would probably have been labeled as having spiritual problems by the biblical counseling standards. They would probably tell these two women who had thorough physical examinations by a variety of doctors, "Your mental problems are simply spiritual problems that we can diagnose and treat biblically, because no 'organically generated difficulties' have been found." After the discovery of their true diseases, the biblical counselors would be regarded as false teachers.

We want to make it clear that we do not recommend that individuals get on or off psychotropic medications. We generally do not write about psychotropic medications, but we do say that such medications are grossly over prescribed and greatly over used. **Through the collaboration of psychiatrists and pharmaceutical companies, psychotropic drugs have been unnecessarily foisted upon millions of naïve individuals. Mental disorder labels are often recklessly and fecklessly applied by doctors to people who are undeserving of them.** Moreover, based upon recommendations from friends and pharmaceutical advertising, consumers request such psychotropic medications from their doctors, and doctors who are on tight timelines too readily prescribe them. There are many skeletons in the psychiatric closet of the past and too many questionable practices of today, including sometimes clandestine relationships between psychiatry and the pharmaceutical industry.

Conclusion

Just as psychological counseling and psychotropic drugs have been erroneously used over the years when no biological illness has been found, some biblical counselors now mistakenly assume that sin or needed spiritual growth are the cause of problems when no "organically generated difficulties" are found. **Just because no "organically generated difficulties" are found does not mean that none exist.** Just because there is no known cause and effect relationship between the brain/mind and many of the mental disorders does not mean that one will not eventually be found. When more becomes known about the brain and its affect on the mind/body and about how various brain activities can affect thinking, feeling, and even behaving, these new discoveries will make fools of those who have been following the either/or fallacy and concluding that the mental disorders are for certain spiritually caused.

We must all be open to the possibility that some of the metaphorically speaking "Mental Illnesses" will have known organic causes in the future, regardless of what remedy is used. The brain, because of its enormous complexity, can have things organically wrong with it that cause mental disorders. Instead of using the symptoms as a means of ministry these ten biblical counselors rely mostly on psychiatric terms and psychological labels, such as "schizophrenia, sexual abuse, eating disorders, bi-polar," and "dissociative identity disorder" as well as depression, to vaunt their counseling victories, but it is totally unnecessary.

Many of God's people have difficult decisions to make. Many have taken the full physicals provided by their clinics and recommended by biblical counselors. They have waited months with mental symptoms. They have painfully gone to work at times and stayed home at other times, doing the best they could under the prevailing, painful symptoms. Their loved ones have perhaps drawn alongside and helped to bear the awful burden of those so afflicted. No one should add to their burden through the use of an either/or fallacy resulting in spiritual blame that does not fit the facts or history.

The best, most sensible position for a Christian to take, even after a complete physical examination that reveals nothing, is neither to imply nor state that a mental symptom is necessarily due to a spiritual problem. But, regardless of whether a brain disorder is a spiritual or biological problem, the correct thing to always do is to minister biblically in addition to any other medical treatment that may be necessary and helpful.

There is always a place for biblical encouragement, counsel, and even rebuke, but such should be done in great humility (Gal. 6:1-3) and with consideration for the possibility of biological involvement. Sometimes the best one may say is, "I don't have a clue, but God knows, and He is faithful to His promises to be with His children (Heb. 13:5), to enable them to endure trials (Phil. 4:13), and to use all for their good (Rom. 8:28-29)." **Christians who desire to minister to fellow believers should** beware of the temptation of becoming like Job's counselors—adding to a person's pain through fallacious conclusions based upon no "organically generated difficulties" or "medical problems" existing followed by condemnation by spiritualizing the causes for most of the 300 mental disorders in the *DSM* plus any others where no apparent medical markers appear.

4

Scriptures Misused, Abused, or Missed

Counseling the Hard Cases (*CTHC*) presents ten biblical counseling cases to demonstrate that biblical counselors can counsel the hard cases under the condition of no "organically generated difficulties" having been found after the counselees have received "a full medical work-up." Thus one would expect the ten individuals counseling the ten cases to be the best of the vast array of biblical counselors and therefore do the very best biblical counseling. Indeed, these ten cases represent the very best counseling the biblical counseling movement (BCM) has to offer and are meant to be examples to biblical counselors and aspiring biblical counselors as to how best to counsel. **However, upon examination we found that the counseling in these ten cases is not only not always the best, but not always to be followed!** The similarities between the biblical counselors and psychological counselors where they overlap reveal sufficient reasons not to emulate or imitate the ten cases. In this chapter we additionally show biblically why these ten cases should not be followed. Add up the educational backgrounds and counseling experience of these ten counselors and it is a wonder to ponder as to how this could happen, but it did! **In the following sections we disclose the fact that important Scriptures are often misused, abused or missed.**

Important Scripture Misused

Proverbs 18:13 is the shibboleth of the biblical counseling movement. It serves as an identifying mark for the in-group, those who have been certified and therefore qualified for biblical counseling through one of their main training institutions or organizations. While nearly all of the authors of cases in *Counseling the Hard Cases* rely on this verse in their data seeking, Proverbs 18:13 was explicitly quoted by Steve Viars in the case of "'Brian' and Obsessive-Compulsive Disorder," Dan Wickert in the case of "'Mary' and Paralyzing Fear," and Stuart Scott in the case of "'Jackie' and Dissociative Identity Disorder" (pp. 69, 112, 207).

When used properly, Proverbs 18:13 is a marvelously instructive verse: "He that answereth a matter before he heareth it, it is folly and shame unto him." Proverbs 18:13 calls for fact finding, particularly when only one side has been heard. William MacDonald says:

> A man should get all the facts before giving his opinion. Otherwise he will be embarrassed when the full details are made known. There are two sides to every question: every divorce, every quarrel, etc. **Don't agree with a person if you have not heard the other person's side.**[1] (Bold added.)

In other words, this verse encourages necessary fact finding, primarily in cases where there are two sides or two points of view. Matthew Henry says regarding Proverbs 18:13 that "when they have heard one side, they think the matter so plain that they need not trouble themselves to hear the others."[2] The admonition of Proverbs 18:13 is then further emphasized in verse 17: "He that is first in his own cause seemeth just; but his neighbour cometh and searcheth him." In other words, if Proverbs 18:13 is the foundational justification for biblical counselors to ask for details, full investigation must include all parties involved in any story being told by one person.

Sadly, those in the BCM gravely misuse Proverbs 18:13 when they conduct their detailed probing, prying, questioning, and encouraging of counselees to tell all so that the counselor can solve their problems in a problem-centered counseling setting. Tales are told about people who never have an opportunity to give their side of the situation. Until the rise of the BCM, Proverbs 18:13 was not used as a rationalization or justification for complex poking around in a person's past and/or present private life. Problem-centered counselors believe that the more they find out, the better they will understand the counselees and their problems.

Human sinfulness is an undeniable plague that has replicated itself throughout all generations so that "we are all as an unclean thing, and all our righteousnesses are as filthy rags; and we all do fade as a leaf; and our iniquities, like the wind, have taken us away" (Isa. 64:6). The verdict is in: the Bible is true. Mankind is guilty! "There is none righteous, no, not one…. For all have sinned, and come short of the glory of God" (Rom. 3:10, 23). Every person born on this planet is a sinner, except the Lord Jesus Christ, who became man to provide salvation from the condemnation, power, and eternal results of this vile condition.

Mary Sykes Wylie, PhD, senior editor of the *Psychotherapy Networker*, which is a publication for psychotherapists, reveals that "most therapists *like* exploring feelings with their clients, delving into family history, helping them achieve emotional growth, going deep—and taking their time doing it. That's why they got into therapy in the first place"[3] (emphasis hers). If we just add the words "plus the Bible," this would describe Scott, Lambert, most others in the book, and those biblical counselors who follow them.

If the psychological counseling movement did not exist and precede the biblical counseling movement, the BCM would not have falsely retrofitted their naïvely psychological ideas into Proverbs 18:13 and other verses to justify eliciting a person's past history in an attempt to know the unknowable. In addition, the biblical counselors speak of things in violation of Ephesians 5:12 and then publicize them in their case histories. These activities would never exist and persist as they do in the BCM absent the "godfather" practices of the psychological counseling movement. There is candidly no precedence in Scripture for this kind of counseling, which adds to our other criticisms making the expression "biblical counselor" an oxymoron for those who practice as we describe in *Stop Counseling! Start Ministering!*[4]

Spelunking, Speculating, and Sinning.

Using Proverbs 18:13 to justify their ongoing emphasis on seeking as much information as possible relies on the idea that, if the counselors learn enough about their counselees, they will be able to understand them and analyze their problems. However, moving from hearing what counselees may reveal to analyzing the counselees and their problems relies too heavily on subjectivity, in which the counselor's own experiences, biases, and weaknesses may distort the understanding. Subjectivity reigns in both the speaker and the hearer. Besides subjectivity distorting information gleaned, any counseling conversation may involve faulty memory, bias, and the deceitful, wicked heart of both the counselee and the counselor (Jer. 17:9).

Probing into a counselee's past relies too much on faulty memory and will not bring forth unbiased facts. Many people still have the false notion that memory is solid and reliable like a tape recorder or computer. Research gives the opposite view of memory. In his book *Remembering and Forgetting: Inquiries into the Nature of Memory*, Edmund Bolles says, "The human brain is the most complicated structure in the known universe."[5] He says, "Remembering is a creative, constructive process. There is no storehouse of information about the past anywhere in our brain."[6]

Medical doctor and researcher Nancy Andreasen says in her book *The Broken Brain* that "there is no accurate model or metaphor to describe how [the brain] works." She concludes that "the human brain is probably too complex to lend itself to any single metaphor."[7] Unlike a computer, the brain does not store every detail as it sifts through the multitude of stimuli during an actual event. Later recall will be influenced first by what stimuli actually went into long-term memory, since a great deal is simply forgotten. Then the very act of recall alters the memory, since recall involves creatively adding details to fill in gaps that are vague. Thus every time a memory is recalled there can be some slight adjustment so that eventually it is somewhat different from the actual event. As Dr. Michael Yapko, author of *Suggestions of Abuse*, says, "Memories are often formed from multiple sources of information and may be modified over time."

Dr. Carol Tavris puts this information about memory in the following nutshell:

> Memory is, in a word, lousy. It is a traitor at worst, a mischief-maker at best. It gives us vivid recollections of events that could never have happened, and it obscures critical details of events that did.[8]

An article about the questionability and failure of memory in *The New York Times* states:

> When we recall our own memories, we are not extracting a perfect record of our experiences and playing it back verbatim. Most people believe that memory works this way, but it doesn't. Instead, we are effectively whispering a message from our past to our present, reconstructing it on the fly each time. We get a lot of details right, but when our memories change, we only "hear" the most recent version of the message, and we may assume that what we believe now is what we always believed. Studies find that even our "flashbulb memories" of emotionally charged events can be distorted and inaccurate, but we cling to them with the greatest of confidence. With each

retrieval our memories can morph, and so can our confidence in them.[9]

Rather than a fact-finding investigation, much biblical counseling relies on the willingness of counselees to tell all **as they remember it**, as happened with "Mariana" when counseled by Laura Hendrickson, "Brian" when counseled by Steve Viars, "Mary" when counseled by Dan Wickert, and "Jackie" when counseled by Stuart Scott. Along with the inaccuracy of memory comes the tendency of counselees to intentionally or unintentionally leave out perhaps the most important information. The counselor will only hear a story made up from an imperfect memory, biased perception, self-protecting exclusions, and other forms of self protecting or self-enhancing inclusions. What biblical counselors truly investigate the facts with corroborating information, such as whether someone did or said something in the distant past, by questioning third parties not present who have been accused or complained about during counseling? Instead of solid facts, however, such attempts at corroboration could further muddy the water with added subjectivity and conflicting biases and viewpoints.

Important Scriptures Abused

Besides the gross errors that can occur in such misguided investigations, the BCM's lopsided understanding of Proverbs 18:13 allows and even encourages much sinful communication. Proverbs 18:13 operates as the open-sesame to evil speaking, tale bearing, self-justification and other expressions of Jeremiah 17:9. *CTHC* includes counseling during which the counselee is encouraged to violate Ephesians 5:11-12: "And have no fellowship with the unfruitful works of darkness, but rather reprove them. For it is a shame even to speak of those things which are done of them in secret." Detailed descriptions of dark sinful behavior are not absolutely necessary, and they contaminate the listener and the reader. While counselors may encourage the expression of such details for understanding or for reproof, it is best for the Word of God to shed the light as it is being taught to an individual. One does not have to find out all the dingy details for the Word to open eyes and the Holy Spirit to bring about conviction. Moreover, writing about such details regarding what another person has done does not bring reproof. In fact, writing about someone's lust in detail in a case description could titillate a reader's imagination, and it is certainly not edifying. All communication among believers should follow Ephesians 4:29: "Let no corrupt communication proceed out of your mouth, but that which is good to the use of edifying, that it may minister grace unto the hearers."

The Bible discretely mentions sexual sins of mankind, whether in Sodom and Gomorrah or between David and Bathsheba or with Amnon and Tamar. But nowhere in Scripture is there an ongoing discussion of such darkness as occurs particularly with the cases of Laura Hendrickson ("'Mariana' and Sexual Abuse") and Stuart Scott ("'Jackie' and Dissociative Identity Disorder"), to be discussed later.

When one reads the biased story-telling and the sinful communication in the "hard cases" presented in *CTHC*, one can see that using Proverb 18:13 even with misguided best intentions can lead to violating other Scriptures, including Ephesians 4:29 and 5:11, 12 as well as Psalm

19:14. **Ephesians 4:29, 5:11, 12; Proverbs 18:17, and Psalm 19:14 are not quoted in any of the *CTHC* cases. In fact, these verses are rarely, if ever, used or mentioned in any BCM books.**

Counselors think they are able to understand the person and the problem and to bring about the correct diagnosis and treatment. While investigating all that is available to them with their probing questions and the detailed stories of their counselees, counselors are still left with having to sift through the counselee's biased, self-serving self-disclosure, unconfirmed stories of people not present, and numerous descriptions of problems, feelings, and circumstances. In addition to selective speaking on the part of the counselee, there will inevitably be selective listening on the part of the counselor. That is, the counselor will be listening for certain things according to his life experience and counseling training and may overlook the most important information.

Even after hours of gathering "data," even if these hours extend through months of once-per-week, fifty-minute conversations, the counselor has only a snippet of the person's life. He cannot see the person's soul. He cannot see the true landscape of the person's life or even the landscape of the person's problems. Counselees are individuals with multifaceted personalities, whose lives are interconnected with a wide array of other multifaceted personalities within vast and varied circumstances. Counselors are also individuals with multifaceted personalities whose lives are interconnected with a wide array of other multifaceted counselee personalities within vast and varied circumstances that will color almost everything that is said and heard in the counseling room.

Add to this the multiplicity of counselees seen each week by the counselor and the subjective mix becomes even more contaminated, especially when Case A seems similar to Case B. Counselors often compare what they do with what medical doctors do in finding out all the details to diagnose and treat an individual. But that is a false analogy, because medical doctors are dealing with a physical body that can be examined and treated, but counselors are dealing with the unseen realm of the soul. Thus counselors are greatly limited in what they can truly know and understand regarding their counselees and their problems. That is why we want to direct all to God. He is the one who knows every detail and uses all circumstances to conform each of His children into the image of Christ.

Problems do not always need to be discussed for one believer to minister Christ to another believer. However, because of the problem-centered nature of present-day counseling, the assumption is that one cannot help other people until all details of their stories have been aired and heard. However, what one really needs to know about is a person's walk with the Lord. In other words, **we want to hear how His Story (the truth of Jesus) has impacted their story.** Much greater progress can be made when the purpose is for the fellow believer to grow in knowing and trusting Christ than when the plan is problem-solving through ongoing conversations filled with the Jeremiah 17:9 syndrome.[10] Problems are opportunities for spiritual growth and mutual care among believers. Problems can be used to motivate believers to turn to the Lord Jesus Christ and remember all He has given them: salvation through His death, burial, and resurrection; identification with Him in His death and resurrection; new life in Him; and all they possess in Him to deal with their own problems of living. Our desire is that believers will realize and remember that they are equipped in Christ to live His life and to gain victory in the midst of problems through Him.

Important Scriptures Missed

Cautionary Verses Regarding Talebearing and Other Sinful Speaking:

One glaring failure on the part of "biblical counselors" is that **they generally fail to begin each counseling relationship with Bible verses of caution.** Since the tendency for counselees is to talk about others and typically for counselees to be involved in talebearing (gossip), there needs to be an introductory caution to all counselees before the counseling begins. In counseling, people talk about themselves, their feelings, their relationships, their problems, and other people in their lives. They often talk about their parents, spouse, children, other relatives, and close friends, as well as numerous other people who are not present. While there may be no intentional lying, the story will be told from the teller's perspective. Quite often the very act of counseling will involve participants saying personal things about other people behind their backs. That often involves talebearing—spreading gossip, secrets, biased impressions, and so forth about others who are not present. In fact, counseling often encourages such talebearing as the counselor elicits details and continually searches for clues as to the whys and wherefores of what is troubling the individual. After all, many problems of living involve other people.

The Bible warns us about the evil of talebearing: "The words of a talebearer are as wounds, and they go down into the innermost parts of the belly" (Prov. 18:8; 26:22); "He that goeth about as a talebearer revealeth secrets: therefore meddle not with him that flattereth with his lips" (Prov. 20:19); "Where no wood is, there the fire goeth out: so where there is no talebearer, the strife ceaseth" (Prov. 26:20). Moreover, the Lord commands His people not to act as talebearers: "Thou shalt not go up and down as a talebearer among thy people" (Lev. 19:16).

A caution against such sinful talk should be given at the beginning of counseling and along the way as needed, such as praying together Psalm 19:14: "Let the words of my mouth, and the meditation of my heart, be acceptable in thy sight, O LORD, my strength, and my redeemer." This would immediately set a standard for the counseling to follow, **yet we have never heard of biblical counselors beginning their sessions with such a precautionary prayer**. There are many other verses that should guide the counseling conversations, such as Proverbs 18:17; Ephesians 4:29, 5:11, 12; and James 1:26; 3:2, **none of which are quoted in *CTHC***. Whether or not Psalm 19:14 or similar verses are used in personal ministry, they should be kept in mind by the one who ministers mutual care, since individuals in need of help tend to follow the usual sinful problem-centered obsession with its talebearing and soon need to be brought to a biblical bridling of the tongue for their own spiritual good.

Quoted Verses to Support their Use of the *Heart* and *Idols* Missed:

Although the horror of sin may be extremely obvious, sin may also remain hidden in the heart, just lurking below the surface in thoughts, motives, and attitudes and even covertly emerging midst mixed words and actions. Indeed, the heart is deceitful. Because the heart is the primary source of evil in an individual, many counselors attempt to expose a counselee's heart and identify idols in an effort to help the person cast off the idols and thereby purify the heart or inner man. The word *idol* with its variations is used 34 times in several cases in *CTHC* with the use of only two Bible verses. The word *heart* is used around 250 times with a number of Bible verses cited.

Although verses about the heart are used, those cited and/or quoted do not direct a third party (counselor) to examine another person's (counselee's) heart. Even though there is a warning about not trusting the motives of another person (Jer. 17:9), there are none that suggest that anyone other than the Lord Himself can truly know another person's heart. In other words, Bible verses that tell one person to analyze another person's heart and identify that person's so-called idols are missing from *CTHC* because they are not in Scripture to begin with. While information about the heart is important to convey when ministering, the words *idol* and *heart* are often used in *CTHC* without quoting from the numerous possible Bible verses. All of the counselors are known as biblical counselors and should be using Bible passages as they apply at least most of the time, particularly here with their extensive emphasis on the heart and idols. This is a major example of the missed use of Scripture.

BCM counselors believe they can discover the thoughts and intents of the heart of their counselees. However, they do so in a way that reflects various forms of insight therapy, in which the counselor attempts to know what is on the inside that is driving present feelings and behavior. Even though they are looking for change in the right place, they cannot know or understand the inner man of another person and therefore they enter a guessing game. Many think they are correctly identifying what they call **"idols of the heart"** by searching for clues through conversation and guessing what is there. In searching for clues regarding the thoughts and intentions of the heart, many in the biblical counseling movement treat the inner workings of the heart somewhat like the Freudian unconscious, just as a psychoanalyst attempts to probe the unconscious. Those in the BCM who probe the "unconscious" of the heart have **no biblical justification for this kind of "understanding the heart."** Instead of moving the person closer to the Lord for Him to work on the inside, they often give their own ideas based on their own perceptions that may arise from their own deceitful hearts as well.

Attempting to understand the inner man and identifying what the counselor may see as idols of the heart can be a futile and even destructive activity, because no one in the counseling room is free of having a deceitful heart. Even after counselors may have examined their own hearts, they will be left with remnants and even whole yards of self-deception. The heart is so deceitful that God alone is able to know anyone's thoughts, motives, and inner attitudes:

The heart is deceitful above all things, and desperately wicked: who can know it? I the LORD search the heart, I try the reins, even to give every man according to his ways, and according to the fruit of his doings (Jer. 17:9-10).

Matthew Poole says in his commentary that the **deceitful heart is "unsearchable by others, *deceitful* with reference to ourselves, and abominably wicked so that neither can a man know his own heart, neither can any other know our hearts"** (italics his; bold added).[11]

The Christian Counseling and Educational Foundation (CCEF) exemplifies this inner-workings-of-the-heart approach. While each CCEF counselor may counsel somewhat differently from the rest, they are primarily working in the direction of inner-workings-of-the-heart. A lengthy article by David Powlison in *The Journal of Biblical Counseling*, a CCEF publication, describes his understanding of the inner workings of the heart through what he calls "**the idols of the heart**," which form the diagnosis and treatment of his problem-centered approach.[12]

In their attempt to understand the heart of their counselees, BCM counselors go to great lengths to gather data about a person's past as well as present. They listen to stories about circumstances and others who are not present. They ask innumerable questions because, they, like their psychological counterparts, believe they can know what the Bible says is humanly unknowable. They justify their prying with a misapplication and misunderstanding of Proverbs 18:13.

We agree with those biblical counselors who recognize the need for heart change in their counselees. However, God is the one who changes hearts. Sanctification, including heart change, is accomplished in the same manner as salvation, by grace through faith:

> As ye have therefore received Christ Jesus the Lord, so walk ye in him: Rooted and built up in him, and stablished in the faith, as ye have been taught, abounding therein with thanksgiving (Col. 2:6-7).

When believers are given new life they have a new heart. The problem is that their deceitful heart continues on in their old nature, which is to be put off. Using the counseling methods of the world to change hearts is much like what Paul warns about in the very next verse:

> Beware lest any man spoil you through philosophy and vain deceit, after the tradition of men, after the rudiments of the world, and not after Christ (Col. 2:8).

Instead of counseling methods of the world or being influenced by them, believers need to be encouraging one another in the faith to be built up in Christ. This is not accomplished by exploring a person's past, focusing on that person's problems, or analyzing the person's deceitful heart of the old nature. True heart change comes from turning one's attention to Christ, who He is in Himself (the Son of God, creator and sustainer of the universe) and who Christ is in the believer. Every problem believers face should drive them closer to Christ, who is their life. Instead, with the modern-day belief that counseling will solve their problems, they often end up focusing on themselves and their problems and miss a tremendous opportunity for spiritual growth.

Value of Trials, Tribulations, Sufferings:

Trials, tribulations, and suffering serve as fertile soil for knowing God experientially and growing spiritually. The Bible is clear about the value of suffering when a person turns to the Lord through it. The entire book of Job is about suffering, knowing God aright, and spiritual growth. **Yet, there is not one verse from Job in all ten cases.** The apostles knew God through suffering. Yet we did not see an emphasis on the importance of suffering in *CTHC*. In fact very few of the Scriptures having to do with suffering were even mentioned. Moreover, those that were used were barely mentioned. **While trials, tribulations and suffering verses are not always needed, it seems axiomatic that with the hard cases they would be mandatory.**

Because the ten cases are presented as real cases to serve as real examples of how to really counsel the hard cases, we expected to see in-depth examples of how the counselees' trials, tribulations, and sufferings are referred to **in Scripture** as a means of teaching them the value of suffering. Therefore we looked at the list of **verses** used in *CTHC* to see if any of the important passages about suffering were there, such as 1 Peter 5:10, "But the God of all grace, who hath called us unto his eternal glory by Christ Jesus, after that ye have suffered a while, make you perfect, stablish, strengthen, settle you." There was one brief reference to 2 Corinthians 1:4, but it was not quoted. Steve Viars quoted Philippians 3:7-11, but did not discuss this verse in terms of the value of suffering. Aside from Roman 5:3-5 being referenced once for something unrelated to suffering, the only person who brought this important passage into counseling was Heath Lambert, who quoted Romans 5:1-5. Kevin Carson was the only one to use James 1:2. Lambert and Carson were the only writers in the entire *CTHC* book who quoted verses that dealt with the value of suffering.

Even though *CTHC* counselors spoke of the value of suffering, their words do not carry the spiritual power or authority that Scripture does. If God says something through His revealed Word, the person connects the words more directly to God himself and is thus responsible to God for receiving and acting on the truth by grace through faith. Even when a counselor is saying much the same thing, it is still the counselor speaking and the sense of responsibility to do and act would be in response to the counselor. The truth would be "once-removed" and separated from the impact and power of God's Word to the person if the Scriptures are not used directly. Believers who minister to one another must remember that there is a big difference between what Scripture says ("Thus saith the Lord") and what "my counselor" says. Reading or quoting the Scriptures is the biblical way to minister. God's Word and the Holy Spirit are available 24/7 and believers need to learn to use their spiritual sword. God's Word as applied by the Holy Spirit empowers the believer to go through the fire of trials, tribulations, and sufferings.

Not adequately quoting and connecting Bible verses with the value of suffering is a serious omission. When people are going through problems and trials, they are in a place for God to work His life in His children. Paul welcomed trials and talked about their importance in the Christian walk for knowing God more deeply, learning to walk by faith rather than sight, and recognizing that God uses suffering to mature His children. Paul provided many verses for God's people to use in ministering to others and those who minister should give them to others as well.

Talking about oneself, complaining about one's circumstances, parents, and others, and focusing on fixing things gravely miss the mark of growing in one's personal knowledge of Christ by "being partakers of Christ's sufferings." While we would not ignore a fellow believer's problems and while we would want to give practical help, we would want to major on the person's relationship with the Lord and coming to know Him more completely through the trial. If a person can learn to walk with God more fully by submitting to Christ in the midst of present trials, that person will not only grow spiritually, but will know where to turn and how to walk through subsequent trials.

Although nine out of ten of the *CTHC* cases may touch on these important truths, with few brief exceptions, they were almost absent from these case descriptions. Overlooking such important truths places much of the *CTHC* counseling into the category of walking and counseling by sight more than by faith. In addition, the repeated misuse of Proverbs 18:13 to elicit information and thereby attempt to know the content of another person's "idols of the heart" further indicates a tendency to walk and counsel by sight more than faith, much like their psychological counterparts

No Scriptures to Justify "Biblical Counseling":

Perhaps the greatest omissions in *CTHC* are specific verses properly quoted within the context of Scripture that might justify the kind of biblical counseling they perform. Scott, Lambert, and others assume that the counseling they do is truly biblical. But, where are the Scriptures that direct believers to counsel in a manner that was not used until after the mid-twentieth century and that closely resembles the way psychological counselors operate? The word *counsel* and its variations are plentifully used in *CTHC*, but none connect Scripture to the typical BCM type of counseling. **In other words, so-called biblical counselors have no biblical support for what they are doing with people.** The same is true for Adams in his *Competent to Counsel* book. While Adams justifies the use of the word *nouthetic* as to his kind of counseling by constraining its meaning, there is no exegetical support for contemporary biblical counseling as performed by Adams, Scott, Lambert, and their followers.

5

Cross-Gender Counseling

Though none of the ten cases involves a woman counseling a man in *Counseling the Hard Cases* (*CTHC*), there are four cases in which a man is counseling a woman alone and two cases in which a man is counseling a couple. The cases of a man counseling a woman alone are those of Dan Wickert, Stuart Scott, Robert Jones, and John Babler. Jones and Babler also counseled women with their husbands. The other cases of a man counseling a couple are those of Heath Lambert and Garrett Higbee. **While demonstrating how to counsel "the hard cases," they are also setting unbiblical examples.** Most of this chapter is a reprint from Chapter 5 of our book *Stop Counseling! Start Ministering!*[1] with slight modifications in relation to these six cases, which violate biblical and practical reasons for not doing cross-gender counseling.

Cross-gender counseling occurs prolifically with men counseling women, women counseling men, and a man or a woman counseling a couple. The bigger offender of the two is the male counselor because at least two-thirds of the counselees are women. And, while licensed psychological counselors are mostly women, biblical counselors are still mostly men. Unfortunately, a male counselor with a female counselee is standard practice among many biblical counselors. **All cross-gender counseling should cease for both biblical and practical reasons.**

No Biblical Examples

We look to the Bible to see what Scripture reveals. As we repeatedly say, Scripture presents no example of what is called biblical counseling as it is practiced today. Also, nowhere in Scripture is there a hint or example of a man counseling a woman as currently practiced in biblical counseling, and nowhere in the Bible is there an example of a woman counseling a man as currently practiced in some biblical counseling circles. There are numerous teachings and admonitions throughout Scripture about life, living, and the issues of life, but there is no example in all of these of any cross-gender counseling. In addition, there is no example or even hint of marital counseling as described in *CTHC*. There are teachings about marriage and the marriage relationship, but nowhere in Scripture is there any example or precedence for the marriage counseling that occurs in *CTHC* and generally throughout the biblical counseling movement (BCM).

Women and Men in Counseling

There are great similarities between men and women; however, there are some significant differences which affect cross-gender counseling. It seems trivial and almost unnecessary to say, but men and women are different from one another and these differences enter into the counseling setting. In addition to biblical differences between men and women, there are biological, behavioral, hormonal, and functional differences.

Differences between men and women begin before birth and continue throughout life. *Science News* reports:

> The reason boys like trucks and girls like dolls relates to fetal differences in brain development, explains Heather Patisaul, a neuroendrocrinologist at North Carolina State University in Raleigh. Males develop differently from females—physically and behaviorally—largely through programming by androgens (male sex hormones such as testosterone).[2]

The *Scientific American Mind* reports in "The Neural Roots of Intelligence" on the differences in the neural networks of intelligence in men and women. They say:

> The specific areas in this network are different in men and women, suggesting there are at least two different brain architectures that produce equivalent performance on IQ tests. In general, we found that in women more gray and white matter in frontal brain areas, especially those associated with language, was correlated with IQ scores; in men IQ scores correlated with gray matter in frontal areas and, especially, in posterior areas that integrate sensory information.[3]

Of course there are similarities between the brains of men and women. However, *Scientific American Mind* says, "It turns out that male and female brains differ quite a bit in architecture and activity."[4] The journal also says that "over the past decade investigators have documented an astonishing array of structural, chemical and functional variations in the brains of males and females."[5] The *Scientific American Mind* produced a special issue devoted to "Male vs. Female Brains" with the words "His Brain, Her Brain, How we're different" on the cover.[6] While this special issue does speak of similarities between the sexes, it is primarily about the differences. One writer sums it up by saying: "There is ample evidence that men and women think, express themselves and even experience emotions differently."[7] Linguist Deborah Tannen explains "Genderspeak" as follows: "Men's talk tends to focus on hierarchy—competition for relative power—whereas women's tends to focus on connection—relative closeness or distance."[8] The differences in the brains of men and women influence how they perceive and act. **These differences are played out in cross-gender counseling.** There are many other gender differences, but we offer only a few more in the following paragraphs.

Medical doctor Louann Brizendine, in her book *The Female Brain*, describes a woman as "a person whose reality dictated that communication, connection, emotional sensitivity, and responsiveness were the primary values."[9] Brizendine's theme throughout the book is that women are different because they have different brains, and, as a result, women are deeply sensitive to emotions and form strong relationships. One group of researchers reveals the following:

> Beauty is in the brain of the beholder. Go to any museum and there will be men and women admiring paintings and sculpture. But it turns out they are thinking about the sight differently. Men

> process beauty on the right side of their brains, while women use their whole brain to do the job, researchers report in Tuesday's electronic edition of Proceedings of the National Academy of Science. They even explain it differently….
>
> Researchers were surprised by the finding. "It is well known that there are differences between brain activity in women and men in cognitive tasks," said researcher Camilo J. Cela-Conde of the University of Baleares in Palma de Mallorca, Spain. "However, why should this kind of difference appear in the case of appreciation of beauty?" The answer seems to be that when women consider a visual object they link it to language while men concentrate on the spatial aspects of the object.[10]

Dr. James W. Pennebaker of the University of Texas at Austin and his colleagues have "developed a computer program that analyzes texts called Linguistic Inquiry and Word Count (LIWC, pronounced 'Luke')."[11] Through the use of LIWC, Pennebaker et al. reveal by statistical analysis that "the way we write and speak can reveal volumes about our identity and character." They say, "In general, women tend to use more pronouns and references to other people. Men are more likely to use articles, prepositions and big words."[12] This certainly affects conversations in cross-gender counseling.

According to some theories, men in general are "better at systemizing" and "women are better at empathizing."[13] Here, too, these differences affect conversations in cross-gender counseling. Counselors encourage women to do what they do so well—being verbal, nurturing, and relational. Women tend to share and converse. Communication, as it occurs and is encouraged in biblical counseling, which is problem-centered, comes naturally to women and can result in miscommunication in cross-gender counseling. In the manner in which they function, counselors appeal to women to come for help. The counselors offer an environment for relationship and for exploring and expressing emotions in a conversational, female-friendly setting that suits women's feeling-oriented inclination to share. Problem-centered counseling provides an environment in which these female feelings and thoughts can easily be misunderstood or not understood at all in cross-gender counseling. Moreover, an understanding male counselor may stimulate romantic feelings in a woman as he listens to her every word with rapt attention. She may romanticize about their relationship and even believe that he has feelings for her as well. At the least this male counselor/female counselee intimacy may well make a married woman's husband appear second-rate in comparison.

The primary reason men should not be in biblical counseling is because their spiritual headship is generally corrupted. It is bad enough when the man's spiritual headship is corrupted by another man; it is doubly bad when it is corrupted by a women counselor. While a woman counseling a man does not happen in *CTHC*, none of the ten counselors have spoken against such a practice as far as we know. In summary, cross-gender counseling is detrimental for both men and women. **The spiritual headship of men and women's relational virtues are often and easily corrupted in problem-centered counseling.**

Oftentimes in counseling what the counselees talk about can be classified under "the lust of the flesh, and the lust of the eyes, and the pride of life" (1 John 2:16) and the world, the flesh, and the devil. These sinful areas are discussed, elaborated, and questioned during the counseling process. In cross-gender counseling men and women regard these areas differently, respond to them differently, and usually speak about them differently. Therefore cross-gender counseling is detrimental to honest and clear communication and can lead to much unrecognized confusion and misunderstanding. He talks as a male counselee and she responds as a female counselor or she talks as a female counselee and he responds as a male counselor. **The speaking, listening, and responding are all affected by inherent gender differences in cross-gender counseling.** The above evidence represents only a small fraction of the support for the existence of differences between men and women that can play a significant role in cross-gender counseling.

"Gender Bias Is Ubiquitous"

Biblical counselors will claim that they preach, teach, and evangelize in the counseling room and use that as a reason for cross-gender counseling. If that were all they did we would rejoice. However, that is not all they do; they do have problem-centered conversations that inevitably involve evil speaking. The evil of evil speaking is magnified in cross-gender counseling, because, in addition to being indwelt by the Holy Spirit, Christians are also living in the flesh, which is particularly active and vulnerable in the context of modern-day counseling. The counselors are men and women living in the flesh, man as man and woman as woman. **Both counselors**

and counselees are individuals to whom the Jeremiah 17:9 applies. Because of this fleshly gender orientation, men who counsel will carry male biases into counseling and women who counsel will carry female biases into counseling, which will affect what is said and heard.

One prolific writer and university counseling professor notes "how much more comfortable a therapist (or anyone) feels working with people who are most similar to her in terms of religion, race, socioeconomic background, and core values."[14] This is very true, and gender identity, male to male and female to female, is also an added strong factor in being "most similar." This is a fleshly factor that also affects biblical counseling.

One academic text on counseling reveals what should be obvious to a believer about a fleshly orientation in cross-gender counseling. Regarding cross-gender counseling, it says, **"Gender bias is ubiquitous."**[15] Research shows that male counselors counsel according to the "male norm." Imagine a male counselee who is involved in pornography speaking to a female counselor whose **flesh** could not relate to it or not have a clue about that kind of lust; and imagine a female counselee who is heart sick over her romantic fantasies about some man and speaking to a male counselor whose **flesh** could totally misunderstand her or not be able to relate to this kind of response. The flesh of both counselors would no doubt be involved in the counseling. **Hopefully no one is naïve enough to think that their flesh is not involved in their counseling.** Those who would say that this does not happen in Christian counseling are overlooking Jeremiah 17:9 and other verses referring to the flesh and self-deception.

While the apostle Paul would give wise counsel to men on an individual basis, such as with his missionary partners along the way and with fellow workers regarding ministry and conduct, most of what we see in his teachings to women, as individuals and as wives, come through his ministry of preaching and teaching to groups of individuals and through his letters to both churches and individuals. Examples of such teachings about living the Christian life are given throughout the New Testament, and Paul's teachings about the marriage relationship in Ephesians 5:21-25 are clear and very Christ-centered. Notice how often he points to Christ and His relationship to the church and how the marriage is to be a picture of that relationship.

Paul certainly did not waste his time or theirs talking about trivial matters. He was well aware of the problems that Christians were facing, but he taught and wrote to all in such a way that Christ was central and with the understanding that the Holy Spirit would make applications in each life. We note one exception in that the apostle John wrote a letter to "the elect lady and her children," but this was not a private counseling session and simply had to do with walking faithfully with the Lord and guarding against deception. This is a far cry from any private conversations resembling today's biblical counseling sessions. **Wickert, Scott, Jones, and Babler, who do cross-gender counseling, cannot point to the apostle Paul or any biblical example of any cross-gender counseling occurring in Scripture!**

Rapport and Bonding in Counseling

In his monumental book *The Discovery of the Unconscious: The History and Evolution of Dynamic Psychiatry*, Henri F. Ellenberger gives a detailed history of the background and emergence of psychotherapy. He says, "Whatever the psychotherapeutic procedure, it showed the same common basic feature: the presence and utilization of the **rapport**"[16] (bold added). If one is to best assist the counselee, rapport is both a necessary ingredient and a common factor in all counseling and psychotherapy. Through rapport a bonding occurs between the one in need and the one who desires to help.

Rapport is often described as a harmonious or sympathetic relationship as can occur in counseling. Some describe it as sharing a world view between counselor and counselee. Others describe it variously as the magic, glue, sympathy, warmth, acceptance, and encouragement that exist in the relationship. Whatever terms are used to describe *rapport*, they are terms of intimacy, which the dictionary defines as "a close, familiar, and usually affectionate or loving personal relationship with another person."[17] And, no matter how rapport is described, for the counselor it is regarded as the most important ingredient for success in counseling. The counselors' responsibility is to strive for the highest level of rapport in their quest for success.

Everyday relationships in the family or with close friends or others generally include some element of rapport. However, the counseling relationship, because it involves a greater emotional intensity due to personal issues, usually requires a deeper rapport in order for trust and confidence in the counselor to be established for therapeutic success. It is at this needed-for-success deeper level of rapport that one can enter the danger zone in cross-gender counseling.

Think about cross-gender counseling with a man counseling a woman or a woman counseling a man where there is deep rapport with a harmonious or sympathetic relationship, including a shared world view, between a warm, accepting, empathetic and encouraging counselor and an expectant, trusting counselee. This type of relationship is intimate and close and is often entered into with a complete stranger or with one not formerly intimately known by the counselee.

Another term that is used to describe the ideal in counseling is *bonding*. There are various definitions for *bonding*; however, we define it here as a close relationship that is achieved in counseling as a result of intense experiences described by the counselee and one in which the counselee and counselor can become emotionally attached to one another. It is one with inherent dangers that common sense would dictate be avoided between the sexes. The end result of such deep rapport and bonding is seen in various studies regarding such close counselor/counselee relationships. One professional journal says, "Research suggests that therapists have a long half-life and remain inside their clients for years."[18] That same journal reports on two professional journal articles on this phenomenon. The first is the *Psychiatric Times*, where:

> Psychiatrist Barbara Young reported on her personal project asking former clients how they'd internalized their therapy. A client from 20 years before, who told Young that she checks in daily

with God about her decisions and feelings, suddenly looked at Young and exclaimed, "He talks to me just like you used to!"[19]

The second is from *Psychotherapy Theory, Research, Practice, Training*, where:

> James Mosher of Miami University reported on a study about how former clients who've been in therapy for varying periods internalized their therapists over time. One client, who'd had eight sessions, described her therapist as a protective shell. "It was like being on *Who Wants to be a Millionaire* and using a lifeline," said another short-term client. After awhile, however, clients experienced the therapist's presence as being inside. Therapy, said one longer-term client, became "something that was deepening in me."[20]

The biblical blueprint for an intimately personal male/female relationship is the godly marriage as described in Scripture where spiritual headship with all its responsibilities and privileges is the man's and where spiritual submission with all its responsibilities and privileges is the woman's (Eph. 5:22-33). Granted that the extent of the intimate relationship in counseling is not the same as in the marriage relationship, it certainly strives for the type of intimacy that occurs through rapport and bonding, which can have serious possible consequences as we describe later in the section titled "Sex and the Counselor."

Should a female counselor strive for rapport and bonding, which could lead to an intimate relationship with a male counselee who is not her husband? Such is not the case in *CTHC*, but neither is this practice condemned by any of the ten counselors in all their writings that we have read. Should a male counselor strive for rapport and bonding, which could lead to an intimate relationship with a female counselee who is not his wife? **The obvious answer is no!** Based upon the absence of any biblical example or exhortation regarding such a relationship, it follows that no such male-female counseling relationship, as occurs with Wickert, Scott, Jones, and Babler, should exist among God's people. Can you imagine the Apostle Paul recommending, endorsing, or utilizing this kind of rapport and bonding in cross-gender counseling?!

"Transference" and "Countertransference"

There are certain common occurrences in counseling that have been observed, named, and described.[21] One of these is when counselees tend to transfer into the relationship with the counselor the sometimes intense feelings experienced with other significant figures in their life. These are very "often manifested as an erotic attraction towards a therapist, but can be seen in many other forms."[22] This is referred to in the literature as "transference." Another, which is related, is called "countertransference," which is when the counselor experiences the total range of feelings, positive and/or negative, towards a counselee.

In his book *On Being a Therapist*, Professor Jeffrey Kottler says:

> Several researchers have urged clinicians to examine their fantasies with clients as a clue to how countertransference may be operating. Whether

these fantasies are primarily rescue oriented, sexual, or expressive of rage, frustration, and anger, **most therapists entertain fantasies and daydream about many of their clients.**[23] (Bold added.)

Because of the problem-centered nature of biblical counseling, these same fantasies are possible with a biblical counselor as well.

Although a high level of rapport and bonding are what the counselor desires to achieve, they can lead to transference and countertransference, with its problems and difficulties, which a counselor would want to avoid. These occurrences commonly happen in both psychological and biblical counseling, but are less likely to occur in the ministry of mutual care. Even though one may disagree with using these terms and explanations, we know that there are intense feelings, both positive and negative, that a counselee can experience towards a counselor and vice versa. Regardless of the explanation for these intense feeling that occur and are labeled "transference" and "countertransference," they nonetheless do occur and need to be considered, especially in cross-gender counseling.

Because such intense emotions can exist in counseling between the counselee and the counselor and because they do occur, we point out that cross-gender counseling involving cross-gender intense feelings should be avoided. Here again common sense alone should dictate that, outside the marriage and appropriate family relationships, these types of intense feelings should be avoided between the sexes, especially in the counseling setting. Counselors often have multiple counseling appointments during each day and throughout the week, with up to 40 counselees being seen during the week. It is amazing that they can keep the details of the multiple appointments clear in their minds **while juggling each unique form of rapport and bonding needed for each individual along with the fallout of transference and countertransference that can occur**. We repeat, all of this occurs in most cases between a counselor and counselee who are usually strangers to one another outside the counseling office.

Sex and the Counselor

Within the "Lord's Prayer" is the expression "and lead us not into temptation, but deliver us from evil" (Matt. 6:13). Matthew Poole says:

> The term *temptation* in the general signifieth a trial, and is sometimes used to express God's trials of his people's faith and obedience, but most ordinarily to express Satan's trials of us, by motions to sin; which may be from our own lusts, James i.13, 14; or from the devil, who is therefore called the tempter; or from the world. These are the temptations which we are commanded to pray against: not that God leads any persons into such temptations, unless by the permission of his providence.[24]

The cross-gender environment is rife with "motions to sin; which may be from our own lusts ... or from the devil ... or from the world." William MacDonald adds that "This petition expresses a healthy distrust of one's own ability to resist temptations or to stand up under trial."[25]

An extremely important reason why cross-gender counseling should not be done, as in four of the *CTHC* cases, is because of the sexual attraction that often occurs in both psychological and biblical counseling. Obviously some situations are more vulnerable to this than others. This vulnerability occurs in both psychological and biblical counseling. In a random sample of members of the American Psychological Association, the *Los Angeles Times* reports:

> Of the 585 psychologists who responded, 87% (95% of the men and 76% of the women) reported having been sexually attracted to their clients, at least on occasion. Sixty-three percent felt guilty, anxious or confused about the attraction, and about half of the respondents received no guidance or training on this issue.[26]

The Harvard Mental Health Letter reports:

> Research has shown that sexual contact with patients is common and often injurious. Between 7 and 12 percent of psychotherapists (psychiatrists, psychologists, and social workers) admit sexual relations with patients. Therapists who treat sexually exploited patients report that all of them are harmed.[27]

The Seattle Times, in response to the question, "Who does the most harm?" says, "More registered counselors were disciplined for sexual misconduct than any other health-care practitioners." They add: "Based on the rate per 1,000 licenses, psychologists rank as the top offender."[28] Because these surveys depend upon the honesty of the counselors reporting, many have said that the figures are no doubt much higher.

Although we do not have statistics regarding Christian counselors, we do have a file folder filled with stories about individual Christians who were exposed because of their sexual misconduct. Irrespective of whether there are statistics on Christian counselors and their sexual misconduct or not, the same dynamics exist and provide one more reason why this type of cross-gender counseling should be avoided.

Men and women may be sinfully attracted to one another in the counseling relationship. For men it is usually direct sexual lust; for the woman it is usually romantic lust. A female counselee who has a kind and compassionate male counselor can develop romantic feelings for the counselor and she may think about him a great deal between appointments. Such tempting thoughts can feed an inordinate desire of a romantic sort—sinful lust. She becomes vulnerable to the male counselor and she may become a snare to him.

A further topic to consider when evaluating cross-gender counseling is the way a woman presents herself in personal manner and appearance. Clearly the Bible teaches modesty (1 Tim. 2:9-10; 1 Pet. 3:1-4) and warns against worldliness (1 John 2:15-16). However, even in the church one can see the influence of the world as women adorn themselves according to the latest fashion rather than in "modest apparel." The fashion industry does all it can to woo women into buying clothing that enhances their sexual appeal. The more provocative the clothing available, the looser the standards become to the extent that even Christian women can be seen wearing low-cut tops, short skirts, and tight clothing. While there is a broad spectrum regarding clothing among Christian women, there are certain modes of dress that would be especially problematic in cross-gender counseling.

A woman's apparel may be a snare in cross-gender counseling, whether she is the counselor or the counselee. If she sports the latest fashion she is a temptation and a snare to other women who might follow her example. She is a more dangerous temptation and snare to her male counselees, who may seem to be hanging on her every word while engaging in voyeurism. Such can happen in cross-gender counseling. Further, consider the possible distracting thoughts of a male counselor counseling a female counselee who is wearing clothing that reveals more than should be seen in public and/or tightly outlines the rest of her body. Under such circumstances he can be tempted to lust and will be unable to give proper attention to what is being discussed. Even if a woman is appropriately dressed, some women's facial expressions and eye contact can come across as sexual, whether intentional or not. A steady eye contact by a woman or man counselor or counselee, which can often occur, may come across as flirtatious or romantic, whether intended or not. Thus, sexual appeal is often magnified in the counseling setting by the manner of dress, mannerisms, and facial expression, including eye contact, during cross-gender counseling and is one more reason to avoid it.

Spiritual Headship

God has clearly established the authority structure of the family and outlined the means by which it is to be followed by Christians. In 1 Corinthians we have the line of authority coming from Christ: "But I would have you know, that the head of every man is Christ; and the head of the woman is the man; and the head of Christ is God" (1 Cor. 11:3). This is further emphasized in Ephesians 5:23: "For the husband is the head of the wife, even as Christ is the head of the church: and he is the saviour of the body." Ephesians 5:22-33 then gives believers the way this is to be worked out in the relationship of marriage with wives to "submit yourselves unto your own husbands, as unto the Lord" and to "see that she reverence her husband" and with the husbands to "love your wives, even as Christ also loved the church, and gave himself for it" and to "love his wife even as himself." Thus God has given the man the headship, which includes both authority and responsibility. This God-given authority has been resisted, misused, and abused by sinful humanity, but those who are in Christ are called and equipped to follow what God has set forth for His glory and their good.

While biblical counselors see themselves as helping couples and families to follow God's ordained authority structure in the family, they themselves violate the man's headship when they counsel a wife or unmarried daughter. Both psychological and biblical counseling are structured to give the counselor a position of authority in the eyes of the person being counseled. Thus it is in error biblically when men counsel women and children who already have a spiritual head. Most of the time an adult woman comes in by herself for counseling and very often she complains about circumstances involving her husband, who is not present during the counseling. In cross-gender counseling she would then be looking to another man rather than to her husband, to whom she is to submit and reverence. If an unmarried daughter is being counseled by a man other than her own father, she is inadvertently placing him in the position of headship. Cross gender counseling diminishes or violates the spiritual headship that God has ordained. It is especially egregious for a woman to counsel a man, who then comes under her authority rather than under Christ. There are times for mutual care in the body of Christ, but here again believers need to remember and respect the man's headship in the family.

A Man Counseling a Woman or a Couple

The counseling of a woman by a man needs to be viewed biblically in the context of spiritual headship. Who is the spiritual head of a woman? As we just indicated, if a woman is married, her husband is her spiritual head (1 Cor. 11:3; Eph. 5:23). An unmarried daughter is under the spiritual authority of her parents (Eph. 6:1-3). In problem-centered counseling, when a man counsels a married woman or couple, there is a danger that he will displace the husband's spiritual headship to some degree, whether or not the husband is present. The types of problems a woman brings to a biblical counselor are often those that should be discussed with her husband; or, if she is not married and at home, discussed with her father, mother or a more mature, godly woman (Titus 2:3-5). **How many biblical counselors even think to ask the husband's consent to counsel his wife or a father's consent to counsel his dependent children?** And, how many biblical counselors know whether the husband or father has agreed to such counseling?

Oftentimes a wife will enter problem-centered counseling without her husband because of his reluctance, but this is also contrary to the headship given to men, because the counselor now functions in place of the husband. In fact, if the counselor is a man, he probably spends more time listening to other men's wives than to his own. What's worse is that the husband of the woman being counseled may be unfairly compared to the male counselor who spends time listening to the husband's wife in a contrived setting, in which he can appear extremely attentive and focused on her. In contrast, the husband may not appear as attentive and focused on her in the midst of their real life situations. Another tragic result of a man counseling a woman is the fact that, absent the reality of the home environment of the woman, the counselor can misdirect the woman's loyalty and submission away from her husband or father, which can result in the counselor usurping the husband's or father's headship. Moreover, too many temptations occur in such counseling circumstances and many divorces have occurred because of them. Also, talking about the husband in his absence (Prov. 18:17) could easily be biased, include talebearing (Prov. 11:13; 18:8; 20:19; 26:20, 22), reveal confidences, and diminish the husband's headship by dishonoring him to a third party. Considering the above concerns, men should **not** be counseling women.

Paul David Tripp, a popular biblical counselor, is a good example of this unbiblical practice of a man counseling a woman. In his book *Broken-Down House* he discusses a marriage counseling situation and says:

> In desperation, she began to seek help for her
> marriage. She wanted solid advice before she ap-

proached Henry again. But it wasn't long before **she was meeting with me alone**. Henry wouldn't come.[29] (Bold added.)

Tripp's meeting alone with a woman counselee has been a regular practice, as he says: "In counseling I have heard countless recitations of men's wrongs against their wives."[30] However, it is doubtful that Tripp and other biblical counselors ever bother to check out such accusations.

Considering all of the writings of the apostle Paul about life and conduct, can you imagine a woman coming to his room for counseling?! And imagine this woman coming to the Apostle Paul's room week after week to meet privately, alone with him, to discuss the kinds of matters discussed in biblical counseling. Or, can you imagine the Apostle Paul supporting or recommending that a man meet privately with a woman at a specified place and time for lengthy conversations about her and her problems every week, sometimes for months at a time? He would certainly not do such a thing as meet with a woman in such privacy for even a moment, let alone hours and hours, week after week! Such private meetings as occur in biblical counseling would countermand his very teachings about spiritual headship over the woman and other matters, besides the inherent sexual relationship danger and questionable appearance of evil. In spite of this total lack of example in Scripture, many men who do biblical counseling do counsel many women, and these men would probably be horrified to think that their female counselees should not be there.

A Woman Counseling a Man or a Couple

In problem-centered counseling, a woman counseling a man or a couple often erodes the biblical role of the man and reduces or usurps his spiritual headship. It is difficult to counsel someone without having a spiritual headship role in the relationship. Biblical counseling is a spiritual setting; there will be doctrinal teaching and it is easy for a woman to usurp spiritual authority over a man in such a problem-centered environment, where biblical suggestions are made, spiritual directions given, and Bible study homework assigned. It is interesting to see those denominations and churches that would not permit a woman to preach in their pulpits nonetheless refer men to female counselors, who are obviously problem-centered and who, by the very nature of counseling, wield authority in spiritual matters. No such counseling occurred in *CTHC*, but neither have the biblical counselors' writings in or out of *CTHC* warned against such a practice.

Leslie Vernick, a licensed counselor, says she counsels "from a biblical world view."[31] She gives examples in her books of counseling men with and without the man's wife present. The Christian Counseling and Educational Foundation (CCEF) has offered her books and used her at their conferences. Ed Welch, the Director of Counseling at CCEF, wrote an endorsement for one of her books. We know of no biblical counseling organization, including CCEF, that has identified the offenders and made a biblical issue of this practice of women counseling men in such intimate relationships as occur in counseling or of this cross-gender counseling arrangement being detrimental to the God-given spiritual headship of men. In an article for *Psychotherapy Networker* titled "Women Treating Men," the author psychotherapist states what is known throughout professional circles. She says, "With my male clients, I became keenly aware that often I was seen by them as a woman first and a therapist second."[32]

The reverse of a man counseling a woman, as we discussed, can occur where the woman counselor can appear extremely attentive and focused on him. In contrast, the wife may not appear as attentive and focused on him in the midst of their real life situations. Again, too many temptations occur in such counseling circumstances and many divorces have occurred because of them. Also, talking about the wife in her absence (Prov. 18:17) could easily be biased, include talebearing (Prov. 11:13; 18:8; 20:19; 26:20, 22), reveal confidences, and violate the one-flesh principle. Sadly, while many biblical counselors would be opposed to women counseling men, we know of none of the well-known leaders of the BCM making a public outcry against that practice and naming those in violation.

Conclusion

Cross-gender counseling creates situations that put both men and women at risk and should not be tolerated in the church. Yet it not only exists, but is prolific throughout the church. With all the biblical and practical reasons against cross-gender counseling, it is a wonder that it still exists among Christians. However, this is one additional look-alike from the psychological counseling movement, which never gave a second thought to there being anything negative about cross-gender counseling. **The biblical counseling movement and four of**

the cases in *CTHC* merely continue the cross-gender counseling of the psychological counseling movement and also apparently never give it a second thought either. We have not heard one leader of the biblical counseling movement cry out publicly against such an unbiblical and foolish practice or name those individuals and organizations involved. ACBC, CCEF, and BCF do not have a written policy regarding or prohibiting a man counseling a women or a woman counseling a man.[33] In fact, we know of no counseling organization that has such a written policy. With no visible opposition to cross-gender counseling within the church, it is no wonder that it still exists. **If this one unbiblical and foolish practice were stopped, it would probably decimate both the psychological and biblical counseling movements.**

6

Ten Hard Cases Reviewed

As we often say, much excellent Bible teaching is found among many biblical counselors. However, what is taught biblically is often undone by their problem-centered practices. Take the ten cases in *Counseling the Hard Cases* to the Bible, cut out all of the unnecessary analyzing due to unbiblical, problem-centered evaluations and applications, and the end result would be at least as successful, depending upon the recipient's desire and willingness to change. These useless excursions merely extend the length of the counseling and complicate the possible cures. Some of the analyzing is more psychological than theological and more man-centered than God-centered. As we have said earlier, one is not able to control what counselees will say, but counselors can choose how to respond to what is said. Affirmatively and sympathetically responding to what counselees say and asking questions for clarification often invite them to say more, which easily leads to murmuring and talebearing. Counselors must decide whether more is needed or more is to be avoided. Counselors can control the direction in which they lead the conversation and, if the coun-selees continue in their own direction, the subject can be changed and the conversation redirected.

Case 1

"'Mariana' and Surviving Sexual Abuse"

Psychiatrist Laura Hendrickson, MD, presents the case of "'Mariana' & Surviving Sexual Abuse." Hendrickson begins with a six-page introduction of "Mariana's Story." Most of the recitation of the rest of the case is a recapitulation of "Counseling Mariana." At the end we were blessed to read of Mariana's recovery and her "Life After Counseling and Lessons Learned" (p. 51).

Hendrickson says, "Mariana and I met 58 times" (p. 30). While we compliment her for her long-time compassion and commitment to Mariana, one is not informed as to how close together these sessions were or how long ago the counseling occurred (p. 51). Such information is important to recounting the case because of the fallibility of memory and the human tendency to inflate one's own involvement. In reading the case over a number of times, we get the clear message that what Mariana's other counselors did was in error (pp. 27-29, 37, 55), while Hendrickson's responses appear perfect in all 58 sessions and she even expresses a couple of self-congratulatory remarks (pp. 31, 54). Hendrickson is at her best when describing her use of Scripture and in revealing how Mariana grew biblically and spiritually. However, we question the accuracy of her retrospective, seemingly seamless memory, with perfect descriptions and perfect depictions of 58 sessions.

We see this in all the details of Mariana's life as told by Hendrickson as she follows the normal biblical counselor's desire to be biblical by following what they believe to be the intent of Proverbs 18:13. Hendrickson has uncovered and unnecessarily reported on Mariana's early family life and the details of her sexual abuse. Hendrickson is at her worst when describing the details of Mariana's sexual abuse. In the first sentence of her case report, Hendrickson mentions Mariana's history of "severe sexual abuse in childhood" (p. 25). She then needlessly reports on the history and extent of this early life sexual abuse, contradicting the intent of Proverbs 18:13 as we have demonstrated earlier. Also, the memory of Mariana in telling her story and the memory of Hendrickson in retelling Mariana's remembering of the story are subject to the same questionability that arises as people exercise their memories, as we have earlier indicated. Knowing that Mariana had already been questionably diagnosed as Dissociative Identity Disorder (DID) and bipolar disorder by prior professionals should have alerted Hendrickson to the possibility of fabrications on the part of Mariana. In spite of this red flag warning, Hendrickson says at her first session with Mariana:

> Because she had been accused of lying by previous counselors, I wondered whether Mariana raised this subject at our first session to see how I would respond. I decided that since love thinks the best (1 Cor 13:7), I would presume that Mariana was telling me the truth in the absence of contrary evidence.... I emphasized that I viewed

my role as coming alongside her as a sister in the Lord, not as an omniscient counselor who could discern truth from falsehood (p. 31).

This is in spite of the fact that Hendrickson knows of Mariana's extensive lying over the years, her past questionable diagnosis of DID and bipolar disorder related to her lying by other professionals, and the well-known fact that counselees lie to their counselors and often for good reasons.[1] Although Hendrickson was wise not to question or contradict at the beginning of counseling, the Bible emphasizes truth—not assuming that a known liar is telling the truth.

Elizabeth Loftus is a research psychologist and professor in several departments at the University of California, Irvine, and "one of the most honored psychologists of all time."[2] Loftus is internationally known for her academic work in the field of memory and contends that in counseling, "just because someone tells you something with great detail and confidence and emotion, it doesn't mean it happened. So just being open to the possibility that you're dealing with the product of some process other than an authentic memory recovery would be a step in the right direction."[3]

Some of what Hendrickson says about Mariana is in violation of Ephesians 5:12, "For it is a shame even to speak of those things which are done of them in secret." We don't wish to quote her from the sections of this case to reveal the extent to which she is willing to go and the extent to which she is in violation of Scripture, but pages 26 and 46 are exceedingly egregious examples because of the details and the depth of the depictions of early life incest. Reading this violation of Ephesians 5:12 will surely appeal to a voyeuristic reader and to the fleshly love of sharing and hearing gossip.

In speaking of Mariana's past therapy, Hendrickson says that:

> … her former psychotherapists were advising her at a time when there was a virtual mania for recovered memories. Numerous books on this subject were being published, many troubled women were convinced they had multiple personalities, and most therapists believed in the existence of satanic, ritual abuse (p. 53).

Regarding such therapy, Hendrickson says: "It is not as productive as it may seem to critique this extreme example of a therapeutic fad since few people continue to practice it" (page 53). Although the satanic ritual abuse therapy and uncovering so-called multiple personalities are no longer in vogue, recovered memory therapy continues to be practiced, with destructive results.[4] This kind of therapy destroys lives and seems to be a major reason why Mariana's past counselors were unsuccessful with her. In fact, one can see that such recovered memory therapy did her far more harm than good.

In her conclusion Hendrickson says:

> Mariana saw Christian counselors who encouraged her to forget what is behind her and reach forward to what is ahead of her (Phil 3: 13). She was accused of making up her history of abuse, pushed to forgive before being given the opportunity to tell her whole story, and discouraged from discussing painful subjects (p. 53).

This indicates the reasons for Hendrickson's violations of Proverbs 18:13 and Ephesians 5:12, as her top priority was to ask Mariana to "tell her whole story." In contrast to other counseling Mariana experienced, she was not "discouraged from discussing painful subjects" under Hendrickson's care. In fact she was encouraged to do so. But, the "whole story" is not necessary for godly ministry of the Word to bring forth spiritual transformation. We see no such examples in Scripture of the "whole story" being required for a believer to mature in the faith. The Bible presents itself as sufficient without the gory details of a sinner's life being described:

> All scripture is given by inspiration of God, and is profitable for doctrine, for reproof, for correction, for instruction in righteousness: That the man of God may be perfect, throughly furnished unto all good works (2 Tim. 3:15-17).

However, drama can be much more exciting to read than doctrine. And, because of one's emotional response, the details of the drama will be remembered far more clearly than the excellent doctrine taught along the way. In fact, case histories containing drama make far more interesting reading.

We know that considerable research dealing with what is called "Post-Traumatic Stress Disorder" (PTSD) indicates that those who receive treatment "do no better than those who don't and that a significant number of people treated...do even worse than those who didn't receive treatment."

> Reporting on the extensive research, the writer says: This negative reaction seems to emerge because, for some people, **the very act of focus-**

ing on their negative feelings … increases their distress and leads to more difficulties, such as flashbacks, nightmares, and anxiety attacks (bold added).[5]

In spite of this, there appeared to be much focusing on negative feelings during Hendrickson's counseling. While Hendrickson reports a success with the reconstructed "Mariana" case, **if others follow the same treatment path, it could lead to catastrophic results for those encouraged to seek relief by rehearsing, rehashing, reliving, and regurgitating their negative feelings.**

Why was Hendrickson successful? To her credit, Hendrickson did teach Mariana much sound doctrine along the way and she made a clear distinction between who Mariana was before and after salvation, but one does not have to go into all of the extensive data gathering to teach the truth. Actually no one knows for sure why Hendrickson was successful with Mariana. H. J. Eysenck, Director of the Psychological Laboratories of the Institute of Psychiatry at the University of London and one of the most referenced psychologists of the last century,[6] concluded from his research and experience that psychological cures were no more effective than the mere passage of an equivalent period of time.[7] This reminds us of the old adage, "Time is the healer of all wounds." Hendrickson met with Mariana 58 times over how long a time period she does not say. Time may have been one factor in Mariana's healing, enough so that Hendrickson's offers of the words of life were heeded and followed.

Also we know from the research that the major ingredient in the success of counseling is the therapeutic alliance, known simply as rapport between the counselor and counselee. Apparently Mariana's only female counselor over the many years was Hendrickson. Is it possible that, because of being female, she was able to develop the right rapport with Mariana and that this alliance was the "open door" to Mariana listening to the words of life?

Case 2

"'Brian' and Obsessive Compulsive Disorder"

Steve Viars, D.Min., says of "Brian" and his "Obsessive Compulsive Disorder" (OCD): "**I have often had the privilege of working with people diagnosed with this disorder**" (p. 59, bold added). Viars contends, "This is one of the common themes I have observed in every person with whom I have ever worked who exhibited OCD symptoms— profound hopelessness" (p. 67). Viars claims to have worked with a number of individuals with OCD (p. 68). Was he successful with all of them? Did he cure them all? We do know that the cures in OCD are not "fully understood," the treatments "may not result in a cure,"[1] and it is a disorder that likely has a neurological basis.[2] In addition, "OCD is a long-term (chronic) illness with periods of severe symptoms followed by times of improvement. **A completely symptom-free period is unusual**."[3] The *Harvard Mental Health Letter* reports:

> Although OCD tends to be a chronic condition, with symptoms that flare up and subside over a patient's lifetime, effective help is available. Only about 10% of patients recover completely but 50% improve with treatment.[4]

The *Psychotherapy Networker* concurs that "OCD is a chronic intermittent disorder that waxes and wanes over the course of a lifetime."[5] Viars says nothing about this important scientific information about OCD.

Without any other explanation or elaboration and in spite of the scientific evidence to the contrary, one is left to conclude that Viars has achieved permanent cures for all of them—**a doubtful conclusion**. Based upon the scientific literature, if Viars has accomplished a permanent cure in this one chronic case (which typically lasts a lifetime[6]) of Brian's OCD, let alone the others he says he has seen, it would be a behemoth breakthrough of monumental importance that deserves showcasing in all the scientific journals. However, our belief, after examining the scientific literature, is that Brian's was not likely a true case of OCD, and probably neither were the others Viars counseled, for which he takes credit.

In his section titled "The Importance of Loving Involvement," Viars is highly critical of Brian's past counsel. Taking Brian's word for it, Viars says:

> Brian's fellow believers had shamed and ridiculed him. At other times Christians had offered shallow counsel, suggesting that he change his behavior simply by memorizing random Bible verses or forcing himself to act differently (pp. 66, 67).

Actually Viars could not know the complete veracity of Brian's statements about others, but reveals many biblical counselors' habit of believing such statements that condemn other individuals not present.

In contrast to the supposed ways others counseled Brian, Viars highlights his love for Brian and says:

> On a few previous occasions Brian had ventured to share his struggles with other Christians, but he had not been treated with the comfort, help, and patience urged by Paul (1 Thess 5: 14).… It was fascinating to watch Brian warm up to the process when he knew he was going to be treated with Christian love. **Within weeks he went from being shy, quiet, and evasive in his answers to being animated, lively, and thorough in describing what was occurring in his heart and life** (pp. 66, 67, bold added).

This transformation "within weeks" is truly amazing and is rarely seen in OCD and other chronic cases and additionally makes us wonder whether this is a true OCD case.

Viars later compliments himself again by saying, "Yes, other significant layers of Brian's life still needed to be addressed, but having someone [Viars] who would allow him to be honest about his feelings was a great encouragement to Brian" (p. 71). Later yet, Viars says:

> It was a personal honor and privilege for me to watch Brian grow in his love for Jesus Christ. I would never trade the opportunity God gave me to help him learn how Jesus replaces idolatrous efforts at self-atonement with a passion for the cross of Christ. Paul told the Romans, "How beautiful are the feet of those [Viars] who announce the gospel of good things" (Rom 10: 15) (p. 84).

Viars refers to those who "fail to grapple with what Scripture reveals as the fundamental issue in every counseling case" (p. 65). He says, "The word 'heart' is used over 700 times in Scripture," and contends that: "The heart is the most fertile ground for biblical counseling; and gently unearthing the spiritual issues lying beneath the surface enables the power of the gospel to shine hope and help" (p. 66). Note that Viars says, "**every** counseling case." The word *every* means "without exception." Therefore, because there are no medical markers for the 300 mental disorders in the *DSM-5*, "the fundamental issue" in every mental disorder, according to Viars, is the heart. This theme is the major force in Viar's counseling. Armed with his misapplication of Proverbs 18:13 (see Chapter 4) to "obtain a complete picture of a person's story and get to the heart of the matter," which only God truly knows, Viars does a psychoanalytic type of analyzing and counseling Brian. Viars analyzes Brian's heart, thinking that he is "unearthing the spiritual issues lying beneath the surface," and counsels him accordingly, just as a psychoanalyst analyzes a patient's unconscious and counsels him accordingly. Jeremiah 17:9, Isaiah 64:6, and other Bible passages would contradict this approach.

Viars' relating Brian's "episodes of sexual lust" to his OCD and then saying, "This was the first time Brian had ever connected the dots between his sexual lust and his obsessions about driving" (pp. 72, 73), parallel the work of a psychoanalyst who often works with unconscious sexual themes connected to present behavior. Viars is a good example of the futility of attempting to discern the thoughts and intents of the heart. (See Chapter 4.)

Viars knows that a diagnosis of OCD is made based upon a variety of factors and that OCD has a multiplicity of faces as the list on the International OCD Foundation website reveals.[7] Yet, Viars gives the impression that he easily identifies, as well as cures, those with OCD, in spite of scientific evidence to the contrary, as can be seen from a report from the *Harvard Mental Health Letter*: "One review estimated that, on average, patients with OCD take more than nine years to be diagnosed correctly, and17 years to receive appropriate care."[8] Without explaining the details or the difficulties of helping and long-term commitment to one who is diagnosed with OCD, Viars gives a biblical means of assisting all those who are thus labeled while ignoring the other known possible factors involved, thus endangering other biblical counselors who will do likewise. Viars says that "those ministering the Word through counseling should be friends of good science and desire to promote the research and development of hard data in every area of human existence" (p. 65). However, after reading this case, we conclude that Viars is neither a friend of "good science" nor promotes "the research and development of hard data." **And worse yet, he has set a bad example for others to believe and follow.**

The best part of Viars' counseling was teaching the truths of Scripture to Brian, particularly the importance of knowing, understanding, and believing the truth of what Christ had done (the "indicative," as in Ephesians 1-3), which enables believers to follow biblical instructions (the "imperative," as in Ephesians 4-6) (pp. 77-78). Guiding a believer into truly understanding all that Christ accomplished on the cross can bring forth the desire and ability to change without the kind of extensive heart analysis Viars unbiblically depends on in his counseling.

Instead of focusing on problems or attempting to expose the heart, a pastor and congregation should be involved in active sanctification, growing in the fruit of the Spirit, learning to walk according to the Spirit with Jesus being the center of attention, and becoming more like Him the goal. The Bible reveals spiritual issues that underlie behavior. Thus it is entirely unnecessary and un-scriptural to use psychological techniques or some bib-lical-sounding idols-of-the-heart methods to gain insight into the inner man or to expose and understand the heart, which is the domain of the Holy Spirit, not of man!

Case 3

"'Sarah' and Postpartum Depression"

Heath Lambert, Ph.D., coeditor of *Counseling the Hard Cases* (*CTHC*), presents the case of "'Sarah' and Postpartum Depression." He admits in his first footnote:

> I have worked with several couples who had struggles similar to the story told here. This case study combines details of these different situations. None of the identifying information in this chapter matches that of the real persons involved (p. 86).

In other words, the case of Sarah is a reconstruction by Lambert of the stories of "several couples who had struggles similar to the story told here." "Several" means more than two. Were there three or more? Were all as successful as the contrived combination of several couples? Or did Lambert take the success of one and stir in the ingredients of all, including those cases in which he may have failed? How long ago did the several cases rolled into one take place, and what is similar about them? Remember that Clark and Sarah do not exist, but are the figment of Lambert's imaginative reassembling of several cases resulting in a refined recapitulation.

Dr. Paul Meehl, mentioned earlier, would label this case, as well as other cases in *CTHC,* as doubly jeopardized with respect to reality. Real cases are literal cases with literal dialog. A reconstructed case is once removed from truth, but a **combination of several cases** into one is twice or thrice removed from the unvarnished truth!

To his credit, Lambert was not counseling Sarah alone, but included her husband, Clark. To his discredit, Lambert is guilty of personally usurping the husband's authority in the presence of his wife. But to his credit is Lambert's involvement of many in the church to support and assist Sarah and Clark. This is commendable and copyable for others to follow, provided that no mention is made of all of her symptoms, as this could legally jeopardize them, as we will explain shortly.

Lambert describes Clark and Sarah's background, including the birth of their baby and the dramatic after effects on Sarah. He also describes the extent of Sarah's symptoms that precipitated the need for counsel:

> Finally, on the afternoon that Clark had called me, Zoe had been crying as Sarah was beginning to prepare dinner. As Sarah held a knife, she began to plan a scenario of picking up Zoe, slamming her on the floor, and slitting her own wrists. At that point Sarah realized that she needed help (p. 88).

Lambert then follows with a section on "The Secular Diagnosis" (p. 90). In this section he delineates differences between "postpartum depression" (PPD) and "postpartum psychosis" (PP), the latter occurring rarely. Lambert explains the usual treatment route that is followed in such cases and comments as follows: "Interestingly, although most psychologists believe that hormonal shifts have something to do with PPD/PP experiences, such a view has never been documented. The only hormonal treatments are uncommon and experimental" (p. 91). Lambert is establishing that there is not a medical problem or he would have said so and would not have written up a case of PPD/PP. To eliminate the possibility that hormones are involved, he makes claims about "hormonal shifts" and "hormonal treatments." To prove his claims, he gives a footnote with three references, the first and third of which contradict his claims.

For Lambert to say that the "hormonal shifts" view "has never been documented" is false. The dictionary says, "Something that is documented has been written down or recorded."[1] PPD/PP symptoms and treatments are well documented in the literature. Maybe Lambert meant "proven," but if he did he should have said so. His second claim that "The only hormonal treatments offered are uncommon and experimental" is also false. "Experimental"? Yes. "Uncommon"? No. The dictionary definition of "uncommon" is "unusual" or "rare." We did an internet search of "estrogen treatments for postpartum depression" and found that they are all "experimental," just as there are many other experimental attempts to deal with many other diseases, but there are too many of them to call them "uncommon." The following is from Lambert's first footnote reference (p. 91), which contradicts his view:

> Seven women with histories of puerperal psychosis and four with histories of puerperal major depression were consecutively treated with high-dose oral estrogen immediately following delivery…. This low rate of relapse, 9% compared to an expected 35-60% without prophylaxis, sug-

> gests that oral estrogen may stem the rapid rate of change in estrogen following delivery, thereby preventing the potential impact on dopaminergic and serotonergic neuroreceptors.[2]

In other words, hormone treatment has proven helpful.

Lambert's second reference supports his view, but is dated February 2003. However the third reference given by Lambert, dated October 2010, does not support his view (p. 91). The reference is to Thomas R. Insel, MD, director of the National Institute of Mental Health. Insel speaks about "research to expand the understanding of the causes of, and treatments for, postpartum conditions." He then says:

> What new treatments are on the horizon? In preliminary trials, 17-beta estradiol, a form of estrogen, was shown to have a relatively rapid antidepressant effect in women with PPD, faster than typical antidepressant medications like SSRIs, which can take up to 8 weeks to start working. And unlike antidepressants, evidence suggests that the increased levels of estrogen associated with the treatment are not detected in breast milk, and therefore presumably do not pass to the nursing newborn.

After discussing two studies, Insel says, "Both of these studies provide evidence that the change in estrogen levels during the postpartum period may be a primary hormonal trigger for PPD."[3] Again, Lambert's reference does not support his teaching.

Lambert has by-passed the recent research and painted a simplistic picture for other biblical counselors to draw from and tragically counsel women with PPD/ PP symptoms who may have biological issues behind their symptoms. One would think that Dan Wickert, MD (OB/GYN), who did one of the ten cases would have warned Lambert about PPD and PP. We can only guess that Wickert, an OB/GYN doctor, agrees with Lambert's conclusion about Sarah being a non-medical case.

Like other cases in *CTHC*, Lambert reconstructs with perfection on what he says and what he does during the counseling sessions with occasional self-compliments on pp. 86, 94, 98, 99, 103, and 110. This sounds bizarre to us, as Lambert took several stories, massaged them into one, gave retrospective words to the one manufactured case and lauds himself along the way.

Lambert says:

> I also insisted that Clark make an appointment for Sarah to see her physician as soon as possible. The Bible's clear teaching on the importance of the body encourages seeking the assistance of trained medical professionals in situations such as this (p. 97).

He also says, "In such instances a couple should demand that their medical providers administer physical exams and appropriate laboratory testing to rule out any organic causes for their problems" (p. 97). **As we have revealed earlier, no matter how much laboratory testing one does, that can never entirely "rule out any organic causes for their problems."**

The truth is that in such complex cases as PPD and PP only God knows whether the symptoms are due to physical changes, emotional factors, lifestyle influences, spiritual issues, or a combination of all of these. Lambert has decided that Sarah's disorder is not due to physical changes. We have shown earlier that this is an error that many may copy to the detriment of the women involved.

Lambert reports that:

> Sarah did go to see her OB/GYN the next day; but unfortunately, the visit did not go well.... After asking her a few questions, her doctor insisted that Sarah seek psychiatric help. He informed her that he would check up on her in coming days, and if she had not contacted a counselor in the next day or so, he would be forced to report her to Child Protective Services. Thankfully, he was satisfied when they informed him that they were already meeting with a counselor, and they never heard from him again (p 97).

Lambert gives his prior counseling experiences with similar situations and then says, "However, I say it to encourage women who are experiencing similar difficulties **to avoid merely reporting their situation to their physician**" (97, bold added). This could be a seriously misunderstood bit of counsel. What is similar? Lambert should have warned other biblical counselors that every state has its own child abuse laws and a pastor will generally have clergy protection under "penitential communication." However, non-pastors will no doubt be required to report all "similar situations" or be breaking the law for not doing so. As we cautioned earlier, if those in the congregation were privy to the privacy of all that was told Lambert, they would be obligated by law to report it.

Since Lambert is a quintessential biblical counselor and a distinguished leader in the biblical counseling movement, he is sure to be imitated and trusted. Many will read his advice to "encourage women who are experiencing similar difficulties to avoid merely reporting their situation to their physician" and advise the same under "similar circumstances," which may be to their own legal detriment, as they would be privy to information that would have to be reported.

As Sarah was recovering Lambert says:

> It was now time to address another area where Clark and Sarah needed to encounter Christ.... I now needed to shift to another area— the ways in which Clark and Sarah had each sinned against God and against each other in their situation (p. 106).

Typical of the BCM movement is the counselor taking it upon himself to confront the counselees' sins. Lambert says: "There were definitely specific areas where Sarah needed to pursue confession and repentance of sin. One area was her responses of sinful anger toward Clark and Zoe" (p. 107). He later speaks of Sarah beginning "the process of confessing her sin to God, to Clark, and even to [baby] Zoe (why not?)" (p. 108).

Lambert not only points out her sinful responses under duress, but informs her that she has had a pattern of anger since childhood and that her weakened condition was no excuse. Whoa! Wait a minute. Let us recapitulate. Lambert says:

> As a child she had a difficult relationship with her mother. They were never close. Her mom

abused alcohol and had a terrible temper. Sarah observed her mother's fits of rage as she would yell and throw whatever was nearby. As Sarah grew up, she began to imitate her mother. Her life was marked by severe fights that would often result in yelling and throwing anything in sight. These incidents had subsided when Sarah became a believer. They vanished completely when she married Clark (p. 89).

As a result of Lambert believing that Sarah needed to repent, he says:

Sarah began to realize that she had never dealt with the patterns of anger she learned in childhood. Instead, they had just gone dormant. When she was living with her mother, Sarah's anger would constantly flare up. While living with Clark, her external circumstances had changed, and the temptation had abated. Now that her temptation had returned, the sinful disposition of her heart reared its ugly head and revealed her need to repent (p. 107).

What we quoted earlier from distinguished professor and memory expert Elizabeth Loftus applies here. She says that in counseling, "just because someone tells you something with great detail and confidence and emotion, it doesn't mean it happened. So just being open to the possibility that you're dealing with the product of some process other than an authentic memory recovery would be a step in the right direction."[4]

Questions: How does Lambert know this description of Sarah's mother is accurate? Answer: He does not know for sure! A whole host of questions come up that Lambert cannot answer. For examples: would Sarah's mother agree that she "abused alcohol" or just drank occasionally? How often did Sarah's mother exhibit "fits of rage as she would yell and throw whatever was nearby"? Once? Twice? Regularly? We do not know and Lambert would not know either! Why does Lambert deal with the distant unknown past, which is completely unnecessary to know, in order to minister to Sarah? This is more psychological than biblical.

The combined case of Clark and Sarah, admittedly assembled from similar stories of several couples, strikes us as a presumptuous unbiblical demonstration, as Lambert remonstrates against this couple. Lambert has mercilessly butted in and biblically battered both Sarah and Clark in his attempt to address their sins against each other and against God. He describes Sarah's sinfulness in some detail. According to Lambert, Jesus was bringing her to a realization of sins of pride and selfishness, but one wonders how much coaching she was getting from Lambert, who clearly confronts Clark with the following words: "You know, Clark, I wonder how you missed all of Sarah's struggling going on right under your nose?" Lambert then says, "This question cut Clark to the core" and comments how "Clark was now realizing that his presumptuous behavior was recklessly selfish and unloving" (p. 108). In the process, Lambert pitilessly pours pious platitudes about his biblical right to do so, without properly parsing the Scriptures and absent of any connection between the various verses he quotes and the reasons he gives for why he should take the one-up position on this (p. 107).

As we say in the prior section on "Cross Gender Counseling," the spiritual headship of men is easily corrupted in problem-centered counseling and the place of the wife is also corrupted by Lambert (1 Cor. 11:3; Eph. 5:22-33). Lambert has unbiblically usurped Clark's biblically rightful place in his relationship with his wife and takes authority away from Clark. In doing so, he in essence becomes Sarah's spiritual head (like a surrogate husband) as he leads her in confession and repentance of sins committed within the confines of marriage with seemingly little sympathy for her weakened condition.

Rather than Lambert unbiblically and unmercifully violating Clark's spiritual authority, thus obscuring Sarah's biblical relationship to her husband, which is sinful in itself, it would be better to encourage them into a daily walk with the Lord and to trust the Holy Spirit to convict them of past and present sins. There is something terribly demeaning to have the counselor engineer the whole process rather than allowing the Holy Spirit to do what He does best. When a counselor confronts any sin that a person has committed against anyone but himself, choreographs what is to be said and done, and then oversees the operation, there is a greater possibility for superficiality than true genuine confession, repentance, and forgiveness. During such times as experienced by this aggregate couple going through the trials, tribulations, and sufferings of life, those who minister must remember the biblical possibilities of encouraging them into a daily walk with the Lord as a means of drawing them close to Him. The Lord can do much better than a human counselor in confronting them with their sins, which is the work of the Holy Spirit.

Case 4

"'Mary' and Paralyzing Fear"

Dan Wickert, MD, presents the case of "Mary" and her "paralyzing fear." Wickert begins the case very well by revealing what was frightening to Mary. The extent of Mary's fears are enumerated as well as her resulting disablement. However, Wickert moves from excellent biblical descriptions to psychological interpretations. Thus he moves away from being a biblical counselor into acting like a psychological counselor.

In Wickert's opinion, and that is all this amounts to, he says the following:

> In our fourth meeting we discussed her craving for **control**. All of Mary's fears— her fear of death by AIDS, her fear of infecting her family with AIDS, her fear of her friends' judgment if she were to contract AIDS—stemmed from a desire for **control**. Mary wanted to **control** her future. She wanted to **control** her family's health and well-being. She wanted to **control** her friends' opinions of her. Of course, our natural desires for safety, comfort, and health are not inherently wrong. But Mary was willing to sin to get what she wanted. She was willing to stop serving her family, her friends, and her church in order to

maintain her safety, comfort, and health. She was motivated, driven, and striving for **control** over her circumstances (pp. 129-130, bold added).

Wickert repeatedly and repetitiously labels Mary's problem as one of "control" to such an extent that Mary later reflects back exactly what she learned from him when she says, "I repented to God that I want to be in control of my own life" (p. 135). There is a well-known fact about counselors and their clients, which is seen in the Wickert/Mary case. The fact is that clients reflect their counselor's or therapist's orientation, no matter what form of therapy. The clients think the thoughts and talk the teachings that conform to the therapist's therapy, likewise for biblical counselors. Thus the more they stick with the Bible, the better off for the counselees.

Wickert has moved from Mary's fears forward to what he believes is her real inner problem, but he should have gone back to the reason for and resolution of her fears, as he so well started out to do. Wickert not only strikes out because of his psychological conclusion of "control" but because he moves to a psychoanalytic-like conclusion about the "idol of her heart" (p. 131). We repeat and paraphrase a portion of what we said earlier about Steve Viars' counseling of Brian with a change of names and gender: This idols-of-the-heart theme is the major force in Wickert's counseling. Armed with his misapplication of Proverbs 18:13, Wickert does a psychoanalytic type of analyzing and counseling Mary. Wickert analyzes Mary's heart and counsels her accordingly, just as a psychoanalyst analyzes a patient's unconscious and counsels her accordingly. Jeremiah 17:9, Isaiah 64:6, and other Bible passages would contradict this approach.

Wickert's excursion down the control/idols-of-the-heart rabbit trail decomposes his solidly biblical understanding of Mary's fears. He diverts from his solid biblical beginnings and descends into a phantasmagorical, psychologically-based solution. He could have stayed with Scripture if he had simply related her fears to her lack of trust in the Lord and helped her to learn to trust Him, to practice thoughtful gratitude, and to pray with thanksgiving (Phil. 4:6). Truly, Mary needed to learn to trust God more than self in her daily circumstances, which she finally seemed to do in the end, in spite of Wickert's psychological interpretation.

Like most of the writers of *CTHC*, Wickert criticizes other biblical counselors. He says:

> Counselors who *prescribe* Scripture are in danger of approaching their counselees in a routine, uninterested, and dispassionate way. They instruct counselees to memorize this verse and to write out that verse, but they don't use the powerful Word as a dynamic means to encounter the living Christ. They rarely delve into the depth of biblical passages, the character of God, the beautiful implications of the gospel, or the nature of the sinful heart that fuels idolatry and deception (p. 118, emphasis his).

Yet a few pages later we learn that Wickert himself prescribes Scripture. He says:

> Scripture memory is a sharp, shining weapon against temptation. Memorizing Scripture invokes the aid of the Holy Spirit—God-on-the-scene in our struggles. The Spirit who dwells

within us has the power to strengthen and comfort and gladden our hearts with his Word (p. 129).

How does Wickert know that other counselors assign Scripture in a "routine, uninterested, and dispassionate way" and that they "don't use the powerful Word as a dynamic means to encounter the living Christ"? Is he privy to their counseling? And of whom is he speaking? As usual, with biblical counselors, accusations are made but names and evidence are not provided.

In his "Concluding Reflections," Wickert refers to "the end of nine months" and how "Jesus was transforming Mary as her mind was renewed (Rom 12:2)" (p. 137). Time is always a factor that works in the favor of cure. It is only one of many factors, but time plus the Word, along with other factors mentioned earlier in Chapter 2, may have been working as Mary did choose to trust God in difficult situations along the way.

Wickert's concluding section again contains solid biblical reasoning and the use of Scripture to minister to Mary. However, Wickert errs in saying, "I purposely avoided all terminology outside of biblical terminology." He is mostly correct but also in error because of his "control" conclusion and his idols-of-the-heart allusion. No matter how Wickert explains these terms, his use of them is definitely outside the Bible.

Case 5

"'Ashley' and Anorexia"

Martha Peace, R.N., in recalling her time ministering new life to "Ashley," was a refreshing case to read, in spite of the fact that we disagree with doing case studies. Although sins related to Ashley's anorexia were identified, Peace kept the emphasis on what Christ had done for Ashley and what He was continuing to do in her. Most of what Peace writes about is what she taught Ashley and the various assignments for reading and memorizing Scripture, for thanking God and trusting Him at each point, and for Ashley to find ways to renew her mind with Scripture. Without Peace analyzing Ashley's heart, a beautiful transformation was accomplished through the Word of God ministered through Peace to a young woman who became willing to respond to God with newfound trust, love, and obedience. While death lurked in the shadows, the confidence that Peace expressed in her Lord and Savior gave Ashley a glimmer of hope that grew into sustaining faith.

Peace's background as a nurse also came into play as she encouraged Ashley to take small steps towards gaining weight. But even more important, she guided Ashley in her thinking toward gratitude to Jesus and turning to Him throughout the day and even at mealtimes for mercy and grace. Peace says:

> I encouraged her constantly to push away her sinful obsessions about weight and food. Instead, she needed to fill her mind with thoughts that were true, honorable, just, pure, lovely, commendable, morally excellent, and worthy of praise (Phil 4:8). (p. 155)

Without psychologically analyzing Ashley's heart, but recognizing that every spiritual battle is in the inner man, not external circumstances, Peace says:

> The ultimate battle was still in the heart, not at the dinner table. I asked Ashley to keep up her "Self-Talk Log," recording the thoughts racing through her mind when she was struggling. In addition, I asked her to memorize 1 Cor 10:31 and Heb 4:14–16, to read daily in the Psalms and the Gospel of John, to pray each day for herself and for others, and to keep a "Think These Thoughts" journal. This journal contained Bible verses, good quotes from a book, or specific thoughts that Ashley knew she should be thinking. I told her to add to that journal each week and to review it when she found herself struggling (157).

The "Self-Talk Log" and the "Think These Thoughts" journal were especially useful for Ashley to notice for herself different ways of thinking and to begin choosing God-honoring thoughts. At the beginning, Peace helped Ashley "correct" the self talk, but later on, as Ashley grew in her walk with the Lord, a later assignment was "to continue recording her thoughts in her 'Self-Talk Log,'" this time correcting her own thoughts instead of bringing them to me for correction" (p. 166).

One of the most important aspects of Peace's teaching was in helping Ashley to know God better. She says:

> Obviously it was difficult for Ashley to trust God over her own feelings and self-perceptions about her appearance. Very simply, she needed to know God better—who he is, what he's like, and how he works. I gave Ashley the book *The Attributes of God* by Arthur W. Pink. She and her mother slowly worked their way through the book. I instructed Ashley to pray before and after reading each chapter and to record thoughts, quotes, and Scriptures from the book in her "Think These Thoughts" journal, looking up any Bible passages that were cited but not actually quoted in the book. After several weeks Ashley's attitude began to change (p. 158).

Peace did not simply teach Ashley about God and about following Him but encouraged her to train herself in godliness:

> I explained to Ashley that this self-training would mean renewing her mind and, by God's grace, doing the right thing over and over again until it became a righteous habit (p. 160).

> I exhorted Ashley to persevere in renewing her mind by continuing to ask God to help her replace her old, sinful, habitual thinking with what the Bible calls the "new self, the one created according to God's likeness in righteousness and purity of the truth" (Eph 4: 24) (p. 166).

As the months went on, Peace continued encouraging Ashley along the same lines:

> We kept talking about renewing her mind, re-claiming true beauty, and seeing through the lies of perfectionism. I monitored her hand-written "Self-Talk Log" and "Think These Thoughts" journal, continuing to guide her through the process of correcting her own thoughts. We continued praying together as I exhorted her to trust God over her feelings (p. 170).

At the end of five months of counseling, Peace says:

> As I watched this truly healthy, spiritually fit young woman drive away from our last counseling session, my heart echoed the praise of the psalmist: "The instruction of the Lord is perfect, renewing one's life" (Ps 19: 7) (p. 170).

Of all the stories in *CTHC*, this one was the most instructive for Christians to consider as they minister to others. One can see the elements of personal ministry come together to bring forth life and godliness in this section. While readers will no doubt focus on what Peace said and did, even more important is what "Ashley" herself did. Although she resisted at first, she did the hard work of learning the Word as it applied to her life, of following the instructions and encouragement given by Peace, training herself in righteousness by choosing to think and do according to the Bible, and finally by growing in her trust and obedience to God. We pray that "Ashley" continues being renewed in her mind through being daily in the Word and that she continues walking according to her new life in Christ by faith, loving Him more each day by His mercy and grace.

Case 6

"'Tony' and Bipolar Disorder"

Garrett Higbee, PsyD, who presents the case of "'Tony' and Bipolar Disorder," is a former clinical psychologist turned biblical counselor. He is the "executive director of Harvest Bible Chapel's Biblical Soul Care Ministries" and "the founder and president of Twelve Stones Ministries [TS]" (p. 309), "which is an intensive biblical counseling retreat center" (p. 171). Higbee describes TS as "a retreat with counselees and those who walk alongside them ('advocates')" (pp. 171-172). He says,

> We pack about four to six months of counseling into two to three days. The people who accept our invitation often come with difficult issues to overcome: **schizophrenia, bipolar disorder**, suicidal to name a few (pp. 172-173, bold added).

While there are various forms of schizophrenia and bipolar disorder, in the main both mental disorders cannot be cured or "overcome" in "a few days." The remarks made earlier (Chapter 3) about schizophrenia apply equally well to the bipolar disorder.[1] If Higbee and those at Twelve Stones Ministries have no scientific studies to support what they do at their three-day intensive retreat to heal such extreme disorders and how successful they have been, they need to stop such boasting about being able to treat such extreme disorders. Promising to treat true schizophrenia and bipolar disorder with any real positive results at all in a three-day intensive retreat would be a miracle in itself!

The Harvest Bible Chapel site states:

> When a counselee needs to be seen beyond 12 hours of free corrective counseling by a staff counselor, this is considered **ongoing intensive counseling**. There is a fee of 40 dollars per hour associated with that type of care. We are glad to continue caring for these individuals/couples in need of this level of care. This intensive counseling is costly for us and the modest fee helps *to offset only a portion of our costs* to run the ministry. Your counselor will let you know if this level of care is needed.[2] (Emphasis in original; bold added)

While the "forty dollars per hour" is the least expensive charge we have found for biblical counseling, it is nonetheless a charge. For biblical reasons we are opposed to financial charges and suggested donations for biblical counseling, as we have stated elsewhere.[3] The moment that biblical counselors charge, they become professional counselors, for that's what they are, and the counselees are clients, just like their psychological counterparts. In addition, Harvest Bible Chapel recommends Twelve Stones Ministries for those they believe need such treatment. The cost is $500 for "a one day-counseling intensive"; but for the regular three-day intensive the cost is $1750 for "a married couple with their advocates" and $1250 for "an individual with his or her advocate."[4]

TS has an annual income of over $400,000[5] through their direct charges to counselees, plus donations and offers of scholarships where there is a need.

Higbee describes Tony and his wife, Lisa's, background and says:

> Tony especially had a desperate need to be self-sufficient, to prove himself to others, and to protect himself. His identity was caught up in many worldly definitions of success and importance; he had an insatiable desire for significance, security, and affirmation, especially by male authorities (p. 174).

Higbee has no basis for this description of Tony without knowing Tony's mind and heart. Such a statement is psychological rather than biblical.

Higbee then tells of how Tony was diagnosed as bipolar as follows:

> Tony had continued living his high-stress life as usual, and **he had not slept well for many days**. One night he was overcome with extreme paranoia, fear, and delusions. He began yelling and screaming throughout the house and crying uncontrollably. Lisa was horrified. She had no idea what to do. She tried to calm him down, but the screaming and crying continued. Finally, scared out of her mind, and with no other idea about what to do, she called 911 (p. 174, bold added).

As a result, Tony was taken to a psychiatric hospital where he spent ten days and was given the bipolar disorder label.

After balancing the relationship between sleep deprivation ("not slept well for many days") and its effect on bipolar disorder, and sleep deprivation and its link to mood disorders,[6] we question whether with this one incident Tony was appropriately diagnosed. Harvard University reports: "Studies have shown that even partial sleep deprivation has a significant effect on mood."[7] The fact is that the less sleep one enjoys over a period of time (Tony "had not slept well for many days"), the greater the possible resultant mood disorder.[8] Tony's meltdown, which included "extreme paranoia, fear, and delusions," followed by "yelling and screaming" and "crying uncontrollably," is not a surprising result considering his sleep deprivation.[9] Add to this the quick-to-label, but often done in error, bipolar disorder diagnosis by the psychiatric hospital.[10] Of course a diagnostic label must be attached to any kind of hospital services provided.

After the hospital stay, Tony's pastor recommended Twelve Stones Ministries and "would ultimately support them [Tony and Lisa] as an advocate" (pp. 175-176). Higbee says:

> At first they were skeptical about TS since they had received unhelpful counsel in the past from kind Christians who unskillfully attempted to provide biblical counsel. They gave general proof texts to help them feel better or solve the immediate anxiety. Unfortunately, they only addressed behavior, situational stress, and reactivity, instead of first addressing issues at a level of depth. Yet their pastor was hopeful that we could get to the heart of it from a biblical perspective, so they agreed to pursue TS for help (p. 176).

This condemnation of past counseling based on one person's perception is unbiblical but endemic among biblical counselors. Higbee, like most biblical counselors, takes his counselees at their word with no verification. Besides that, noting past failed counseling enhances the seeming success of the present counseling if it occurs.

Higbee notes a great need for medical testing and concludes, "A medical evaluation and tests, however, showed that none of Tony's issues were conclusively caused by any medical condition" (p. 177). As we demonstrate in Chapter 3, no one can say "conclusively" that Tony's issues were not caused by "a medical condition." In spite of this, after a look into other factors, including "prescription and nonprescription drugs," Higbee says:

> After ruling out any physical origin of his mood swings and determining the impact of other physical and/or situational factors influencing Tony's mental and emotional state, we began to listen for themes in his story that would point to heart issues (p. 177).

Higbee, like many other counselors, is high on heart themes, as he uses the word "heart" over forty times! We discuss the biblical error of such teaching in the earlier critique of Steve Viars' case.

One month after Tony's "night of terror," Tony and Lisa arrive at TS with their pastor, who would be their advocate. Higbee describes the three-day (Friday through Sunday) activities. The major emphasis at TS was Tony and Lisa's "Life Story" (pp. 180-181) and "Heart Themes" (pp. 184-185). Higbee says, "The past is also a crucial element of knowing a person" (p. 180).

On the one hand, one cannot prevent counselees from going into their past because that's what they think they must do by modern standards in our psychological society. On the other hand, it is entirely unnecessary for the counselor to follow them. Higbee malpractices Proverbs 18:13, as we discuss in Chapter 4, and needlessly launches into Tony and Lisa's past, while quoting Proverbs 20:5, "Counsel in a man's heart is deep water; but a man of understanding draws it out" (p. 180), to justify his plummeting into the spiritual heart that no one truly knows or can accurately plumb except God.

The counseling Tony received was the usual mixed bag of fleshly and biblical understandings and repeats some of Higbee's earlier words.

> Fear drove his impulsivity, which led to consequences, which led to feelings of guilt and sadness. Another issue was Tony's performance-based faith, which could possibly be motivating him to perform for us. The more prominent motives or idolatrous lusts that became apparent as we walked through Tony's story graphically on the whiteboard were his insatiable desire for significance, security, and affirmation—by male authorities (p. 182).

The following phrases from the above quote are psychologically loaded expressions: "fear of man"; "impulsivity" leading to "guilt and sadness"; "performance based faith, which could possibly be motivating him to perform for us"; "insatiable desire for significance, security, and affirmation—by male authorities." More of the same is on pp. 184-185, where Higbee discusses "Four

Common Heart Themes" and then teaches about "Anger," "Foolishness," "Despair," and "Fear." He says:

> Anger—The person characterized by an angry heart has a propensity to make an idol of power, control, having his own way, or to be covetous.

> Foolishness—The person characterized by a foolish heart has a propensity to make an idol of escape, pleasure, self-sufficiency, or self-gratification.

> Despair—The person characterized by a despairing heart has a propensity to make an idol of easing pain, feeling good, and creating comforts.

> Fear—The person characterized by a fearful heart has a propensity to make an idol of security, perfection, or looking better than he is.

The above not only lacks biblical justification, but sounds more like left-over psychological baggage on the part of Higbee. He expands each description of the "Four Common Heart Themes" from his past psychological involvement to the detriment of others.

Higbee speaks of "Going Home" (p. 192) after the TS weekend and says of Tony and his wife, Lisa, "We developed a spiritual action plan with the following elements that included the feedback of both the couple and the advocate," Tony's pastor (p. 192). Higbee's action plan involves the following:

> We suggested that Tony and Lisa take time to walk together, to pray together two or three times per week, to **have sex regularly (two times per week for them), and to ask themselves honestly, "Who is in between us figuratively**

> **in the marriage bed? Is anyone competing for our affections?"** The leaving-and-cleaving issues were not so much literal interference as family of origin issues they both carried into the marriage (pp. 192-193, bold added).

And, of course biblical counselors must check up afterwards on the homework assigned! As we have noted earlier in Chapter 4, this is a notoriously unbiblical excursion into the marriage bed, which is not only a serious strike against Higbee, but an additional unbiblical blow against TS and stands as a criticism of Scott and Lambert as the editors. However, this getting into the marriage bed of a couple is not unusual for biblical counselors.[11]

Higbee states, "The counselees received 16 hours of biblical counseling over a three-day period" (p. 194). As we evaluate what was done during those 16 hours and the cost, we conclude that there are better, non-expensive ways to minister to those who go through a similar meltdown with less potential danger of a possible severe relapse. Higbee's profoundly puffing TS is a departure from the other nine cases. While other ministries and books are referred to by the other nine in passing, no one gives details to the extent that Higbee does. Because his extensive, prolific promotion of TS opens the door for others to go there, we believe a warning is imperative. **Very simply: do not believe Higbee's advertising and promotion based solely on his say-so and watch out for his psychologizing of the faith.**

Case 7

"'Jackie' and Dissociative Identity Disorder"

Stuart Scott, DMin, lead editor of *CTHC*, presents a case labeled "'Jackie' and Dissociative Identity Disorder." Scott indicates that he first met Jackie "where I first pastored as a young man" (p. 199). At the end of the case Scott refers to "27 years after the fact" (p. 225). He apparently met Jackie almost 30 years ago and counseled her at that time.

As we demonstrated earlier, a man, Scott, should not be counseling a woman, as it sets an unbiblical example for others to follow. Thankfully, his wife was often, but not always, present. Another unbiblical example set by Scott is discussing Jackie's sexual sins of lust, including her more than "three year [Lesbian] relationship" (p. 201). As we have earlier expressed, such detail is unnecessary and is in violation of Ephesians 5:12.

Scott says, "My first priority was to shine some hope into the situation." What he said to Jackie regarding his first priority was biblically sound. However, he next says:

> My second priority was to learn all I could about Jackie's life. What was her story? Wisdom speaks clearly in Prov 18:13: "The one who gives an answer before he listens—this is foolishness and disgrace for him." I needed to listen well before I

could counsel well. Here is Jackie's own lengthy personal account, which I gained through the data-gathering process early in our counseling (p. 207).

Jackie's story in her own words follows for about six pages. After this, Scott misuses Proverbs 18:13 by enumerating a number of areas he explored deeply with Jackie. Consider what might be going on in Scott's mind as Jackie describes the details of her "three-year [Lesbian] relationship" as well as her other sexual sins and lusts (p. 216).[1] Proverbs 18:13 does not justify digging into a person's past: such excursions glaringly reflect the psychological counseling movement that sets the example and leads to a transgression of Ephesians 5:12, as we discussed earlier.

As an example of this fossicking about for gems in the person's past persona, Scott says:

> In our early sessions together, Jackie and I discussed most of the dynamics surrounding her life story. I investigated her family relationships more deeply. I explored her interaction with the trials in her life, including how the tragic car accident changed her life so dramatically. We talked about her understanding of God and the spiritual steps she tried to take along her path. I looked for evidence of her goals in life and took note of the sins in which she was currently engaged. I questioned her more carefully about exactly how she related to others in her life, and I began to ask myself what God says about each of the key discoveries I learned (p. 213).

It is true that the one who ministers cannot control what a person in need will say. However, the one who helps does have total control over what is said in response. One should not misuse Proverbs 18:13 to dig, dig, dig deeper "through the data-gathering process early" on in counseling as Scott did. What we say may come as a shock to Scott and those in the BCM, but he only needed to follow his first priority with Jackie and not misuse Proverbs 18:13 to follow his second priority to ferret out her memories. The idea that one cannot help an individual in need by following Scott's first priority without his second one is a major, major mistake of the BCM!

What Scott did best was to teach Jackie essential biblical truths that she had evidently missed through her life of deception. However, this should have been done by a godly woman in his congregation, who could teach her about the essence of the Christian life and then guide her along the lines of spiritual growth. Scott did have a couple of mature women in the faith who came alongside to help Jackie, which was far better than to exclusively spend time alone with her as she described her lusts.

Scott alleges that Jackie's story is about her "Dissociative Identity Disorder" (DID). He says, "A number of factors led Jackie's psychiatrist to give her the DID label" (p. 204). Psychiatrists' diagnoses are questionable to begin with, and it is axiomatic that they become more doubtful the more complex they are, such as DID. A recent summary of the results of a scientific paper on DID, states:

> In other words, dissociative identity disorder is
> neither generally accepted in the scientific com-

munity nor has it been well researched by its proponents.[2]

Scott knows that "DID is one of the most controversial psychiatric disorders with no clear consensus regarding its diagnosis or treatment."[3] He knows that DID "may be created through the power of suggestion" (p. 218) and that some believe "that DID is a therapy-induced phenomena" (p. 219) and has provided many footnotes to support the doubtfulness of the disorder. Scott apparently knew that it was doubtful that Jackie was afflicted by DID. Since he knew this, why does he spend a whole special section on "Dissociative Identity Disorder" and why did he title his case "'Jackie' and Dissociative Identity Disorder"? The fact that Scott, a biblical counselor, counseled Jackie indicates that he believed that she had symptoms absent a bodily illness and that her symptoms certified she was DID, a doubly doubtful disorder. The DID label in the title to the case is a false façade used to facilitate the idea that biblical counselors can minister to such a hard case, which adds another active accolade to their actions.

Scott's leaping from the doubtfulness of the DID diagnosis to take credit for a DID case is a catastrophe in the making. Think of all the aspiring and practicing biblical counselors who will be convinced and believe that Dr. Stuart Scott, a seminary professor, cured Jackie, who for certain had a Dissociative Identity Disorder, by the use of biblical counseling!

Scott and Lambert coauthored the "Preface" to the book and mention on page one that the hard cases are "some of the most serious diagnoses," one of which is "dissociative identity disorder" (p. xi). In addition, Lambert mentions again in the "Introduction" the hard case of "dissociative identity disorder," for which he says, "the Bible is sufficient" (p. 24). This apparently refers to Scott's claimed cure. Added to Scott's claimed cure is a concurrence of the cure by Lambert, which doubles the ante of anticipation and participation by others for imitation.

The other two places DID are mentioned are when psychiatrist Dr. Laura Hendrickson describes her case report on "Mariana." Hendrickson reports that Mariana had "received psychotherapy for dissociative identity disorder for 20 years" (p. 25) and that Dr. Ergenbreit had "diagnosed her with DID" (p. 28). Later Mariana was diagnosed as "bipolar disorder." Hendrickson describes some of the details of Mariana's treatments. However, at no time did Hendrickson diagnose Mariana with DID or bipolar. It is doubtful that Hendrickson would certify as a psychiatrist that Mariana was DID, a doubtful diagnosis, or claim she cured her of it.

Hendrickson did say, "I told Mariana that her real problem was not mental illness but an inadequate understanding of what Christ had accomplished on her behalf through his sinless life and substitutionary death." (p. 32). Hendrickson later says:

> We talked about the feeling that there were many people inside of her, and I reminded her that although this was a powerful metaphor that captured her emotional pain, the Bible tells us always and everywhere that we are one person, not many personalities in one body. I continued to address my counsel solely to her as a whole person and never asked her to manifest any of her "alters."

Over time she abandoned the use of this metaphor to describe her internal state. **Today Mariana says that she never had multiple personalities until they were "discovered" through hypnosis** (pp. 35-36, bold added).

Instead of DID, Hendrickson diagnosed Mariana as an "abuse survivor." Thus the title of the case is "Mariana and Surviving Sexual Abuse." Hendrickson's exact diagnosis is as follows: "Like most abuse survivors Mariana struggled with guilt and shame" (p. 32). So, Scott and Lambert's only example of DID is the Jackie case report by Scott, which is based on a doubtful diagnosis about "one of the most controversial psychiatric disorders."

Case 8

"'Jason' and Homosexuality"

Rather than treating Jason as someone who is different, Kevin Carson, D.Min., saw him as a brother in Christ, struggling with a life dominating sin. Jason had grown up in a church and knew what the Bible says about homosexuality. Carson says that during the first meeting Jason "explained his goal for counseling" in these words:

> Since it's a sin and God doesn't like it, I don't want to struggle with this anymore. I want to be happy and to feel good, but I don't want to sin or to think about what God doesn't want me to think about (p. 227).

Jason does not want to sin, but he wants to be happy and he has found happiness and acceptance in relation to other men with the same propensity. In addition he had become involved viewing pornography.

As he relates Jason's story, Carson mentions how he believes that the contemporary culture would explain Jason's problem, but says that he sets that aside and chooses to deal with him as a fellow sinner who responds to influences and pressures with a sinful heart (p. 231). Carson summarizes what he tried to avoid as he ministered to a fellow believer:

> As I began with Jason, I could not let contempo-
> rary culture, personal experiences with others, a
> **limited knowledge of Scripture**, a lack of un-
> derstanding about Jason's specific sins, failure
> to see my own susceptibility to sin, or an under-
> estimating of the possibility of real change keep
> me from **ministering God's Word effectively** to
> this struggling soul (p. 238, bold added).

We wonder how, with "a limited knowledge of Scripture," Carson could be "ministering God's Word effec-
tively."

From Carson's description of Jason, one can tell that
there was a good deal of complaining about circumstances and people. Much of the BCM data gathering is
loaded with complaints about circumstances and other
people. Problem-centered counseling draws forth much
murmuring and complaining, in direct opposition to the
Scriptural admonition against murmuring. Immediately
after Paul declares, "For it is God which worketh in you
both to will and to do of his good pleasure," he says "Do
all things without murmurings and disputing" (Php 2:13-
14). It is one thing to cry out to God, as David did so
many times in Psalms; it is quite another thing to com-
plain or murmur to one another, which is what happened
in the case of Jason. However, to Carson's credit, when
hearing Jason's comments about other pastors, Carson
says, " Of course, the counselor often hears only one side
of the story, and someone struggling with homosexual
desires will certainly be extremely sensitive to any remarks about homosexuality coming from the church"
(p. 236). If any other counselor of the ten cases realized
that they were only hearing one side of the story, they

did not mention it, but rather seemed to take everything as valid data. Nevertheless Carson did follow the usual BCM with his "many questions and extended listening" (p. 242).

On the other hand, Carson did seem to spend much time on bringing Scripture to bear on Jason's struggles and failures. In fact, failures seemed to dominate near the beginning, but Carson explained that struggling with sin takes perseverance. Carson says:

> I wanted Jason to know that we were not looking for God to work some kind of magic that would make his significant pressures disappear over-night. Instead, God promised that throughout the long journey of growth, he would provide grace equal to every challenge. So if Jason were will-ing, I was committing to walk the path with him and to help him through the process of bearing this burden (p. 242).

In addition Jason was to keep a "Temptation Journal" in which he was to record what he was struggling with, what he was thinking and feeling at the time, whether he resisted or not, and how he responded. Carson says that this was for the purpose of Jason "observing and in-vestigating his own heart." In emphasizing the heart and desires, Carson contends "that changing behavior alone is *behavior modification*, yet heart change leading to behavior change is *sanctification*" (p. 249, emphasis in original). Thankfully we did not see a list of idols Jason was to identify, as often happens in much biblical coun-seling. Instead, Jason was assigned to reflect on Mark 7:20-13, in which Jesus talks about the heart as the origin of all sorts of evil.

Each meeting seemed to begin with admission of failure in the face of temptation, yet there was encouragement to keep on going towards the goal of pleasing God. At one point, when Jason thought he may have been exposed to a sexually transmitted disease (STD), Carson says:

> We both wept together as we considered the devastation of sin and how easy it is to be ensnared. Yet once again, in the providence of God, Jason's sin provided the perfect opportunity to discuss the passage he had just been considering. His circumstances over the past several weeks allowed for an excellent illustration of the principle laid out in James: "No one undergoing a trial should say, 'I am being tempted by God.' For God is not tempted by evil, and He himself doesn't tempt anyone. But each person is tempted when he is drawn away and enticed by his own evil desires. Then after desire has conceived, it gives birth to sin, and when sin is fully grown, it gives birth to death" (1:13–15) (pp. 250-251).

Carson's heartfelt response to Jason's failure sounds like true biblical ministry with both the compassion and the truth of Christ—love in mercy and truth. Thus, Jason was to learn something about who or what he would have reign in his heart, Christ or his own desires (lust).

In his final section titled "Jason's Progress," Carson says:

> I still have the privilege of working with Jason but now as a brother and friend in Christ more than as a counselee. I wish I could say that my friend has never struggled since the occasions

recounted in this chapter, but that is not the case (p. 254).

But then, Carson says:

Jason has also grown in his understanding of the gospel and in his love for Christ. In a recent conversation I asked him how his struggle was going. To my delight we talked for 30 minutes as he expressed many different pressured-filled situations, but same-sex attraction never came up. It was not even on his mind as one of his most pressing struggles, and I sensed no need to bring it up either (p. 255).

The best part of Carson's report is that Jason has been growing in his understanding of the gospel and in his love for Christ. However, while one may assume that the absence of conversation about sexual lust indicates victory over this issue in Jason's life, it remains an assumption. It is an argument from silence.[1] No evidence of change in that area was presented, so there is a question of whether this was truly an end of the lust and therefore a successful case according to the overall claims of *CTHC*.

While we appreciate Carson's apparent kindness shown to Jason, there are statements made by Carson that add up to extreme biblical error. The first statement is: "The greater context of 1 Cor. 10 suggests that from God's vantage point committing sexual immorality is no more immoral than complaining (v.10)" (p. 234). 1 Corinthians 10:10 states: "Neither murmur ye, as some of them also murmured, and were destroyed of the destroyer." The apostle Paul is referring here to the sin of Korah, Dathan, and Abiram (Num. 16:14-47), who led a revolt against Moses in direct rebellion against God Himself. Numbers 16:33 says: "They, and all that appertained to them, went down alive into the pit, and the earth closed upon them: and they perished among the congregation." Paul lets the reader know the practical application, which is that such events are examples for our "admonition" (1 Cor. 10:11), and just two verses earlier Paul says." Neither let us commit fornication, as some of them committed, and fell in one day three and twenty thousand" (1 Cor. 10:8). Yes, in the context of 1 Corinthians 10 and Numbers 16, the sin of fornication brought forth death just as the sin of murmuring against God. But this verse is talking about something much more serious than everyday complaining. The murmuring in Numbers 16 is in direct rebellion against God and His appointed order for the children of Israel, just as homosexual sins reveal rebellion against God's created order.

Carson is correct in that the sin of Korah, Dathan, and Abiram was a sin unto death, just as is the sin of homosexuality (Lev. 20:13), but he is in total error that in either the Old Testament or the New Testament the sin of murmuring, which led to the death of Korah et al., is the same as everyday complaining. Paul's warning is about murmuring against God and God's anointed leader to the point of utter rebellion. It is doubtful, knowing the verses in the Old Testament about homosexuality, that Moses would even suggest or imply that "from God's vantage point committing sexual immorality is no more immoral that complaining."

First Corinthians 6 is very specific about the lost who are involved in a variety of sinful living:

> Know ye not that the unrighteous shall not inherit
> the kingdom of God? Be not deceived: neither
> fornicators, nor idolaters, nor adulterers, nor ef-
> feminate, nor abusers of themselves with man-
> kind, nor thieves, nor covetous, nor drunkards,
> nor revilers, nor extortioners, shall inherit the
> kingdom of God. And such **were** some of you:
> but ye are washed, but ye are sanctified, but ye
> are justified in the name of the Lord Jesus, and
> by the Spirit of our God (1 Cor. 6:9-11, bold add-
> ed).

Notice how Paul says, "And such were some of you" (past tense). Homosexual sins are not beyond the possibility of salvation by grace through faith. Neither are homosexual sins outside the possibility of forgiveness, but they are very serious. There is hope for the homosexual, not only in the passage above, but also in just a few verses beyond the reference to murmuring. Paul sets forth God's promise regarding temptation:

> There hath no temptation taken you but such as
> is common to man: but God is faithful, who will
> not suffer you to be tempted above that ye are
> able; but will with the temptation also make a
> way to escape, that ye may be able to bear it (1
> Cor. 10:13).

Indeed, this promise of God applies to all believers in all circumstances, in all temptations. Therefore, if a person continues to have lustful temptations after he is saved, God says that he will enable the person to escape, not through indulging in the lust but by turning to the Lord, who has given him power over sin with the new life in Christ (Rom. 8).

Carson later says, "What I want you to hear is not that homosexuality is not less of a sin but that homosexuality is another sin—one among many" (p. 255). Carson's casual remark about homosexual sin simply being "one among many" is a corruption of the biblical teaching about the sins of homosexuality. He says "Jesus Christ died on the cross for those who engage in homosexual sins, just as he died to pay the penalty for gossips, complainers, and speeders" (p. 255). Yes, it is true that "Jesus Christ died on the cross for those who engage" in the sins listed, but homosexual sins are in a different category than those of "gossips, complainers, and speeders." Homosexual sins are sins against the body (1 Cor. 6:15-20) and against the divine order of the family, whereas gossips and complainers, as long as they are not involved in rebellious murmuring against God, are in a different category. His comparison with the sin of "speeders" would be in reference to Romans 13:1-2: "Let every soul be subject unto the higher powers. For there is no power but of God: the powers that be are ordained of God. Whosoever therefore resisteth the power, resisteth the ordinance of God: and they that resist shall receive to themselves damnation." Such would apply to jaywalking and watering grass at the wrong time of day during drought season. While all sins would lead unto death without the cross of Christ, there is obviously a great difference between the homosexual sins and the sin of driving 1 mile an hour over the speed limit.

A Christian should not unwisely unload everything in the face of one who has entered that satanic web of deception, but the Christian should speak the truth in love, gently, and according to the Lord's leading and timing.

Carson certainly recognized that those who are LGBT (Lesbian, gay, bisexual, transgender) need to hear the Gospel and believe in Jesus and receive new life. Then they will be ready to obey what God says about sexual sin, as Jason appeared to be doing.

Carson expresses his point of view about ministering to those in homosexual sin as follow: "When we stop to minister to someone like Jason, we must be vigilant to see his sin for what it really is—not what culture teaches, not what our previous life experience suggests, and not what a limited scriptural understanding tempts us to believe" (p. 255). **While this is a good goal, Carson appears to have a somewhat culturally tainted view that limits a "scriptural understanding."**

Case 9

"'Julie' and Addictions and Adultery"

Robert D. Jones, D Min, alerts the reader that "many components in [Julie's] story are composites from other cases" (p. 258). Similar to Heath Lambert's case of "Sarah," this one case is a reconstruction "from other cases." Rolling several "composites from other cases" into one allows Jones to pick and choose "from other cases" to create the resulting case of "Julie." This allows Jones, as it did for Lambert, the latitude to liberally assemble a case much to his liking.

Jones became "a lead pastor at age 26" (p. 257) and the Julie case, which includes her husband, Nate, dates back to that time. He says, "I encountered it relatively early in my ministry," and, "The case took over two years from start to finish (p. 258). We assume that all the other cases which helped to form the composite also occurred early in his ministry as well. Now the question is: how many years ago was this, as time would affect the accuracy and possible fallacy of the reconstruction by memory as we discussed earlier?

Jones says that as a young pastor, "what I feared most was facing a difficult counseling situation" (p. 257). He says further:

> In one sense my concern was unavoidable. Based on Scripture, I believed that my pastoral call-

ing included counseling— that a shepherd must shepherd his members through their fears, conflicts, despair, sinful habits, and a host of other problems (p. 258).

This ongoing, prevalent, and erroneous idea that all pastors have a God-given, biblically-based responsibility to counsel we debunk in a later chapter. Suffice it to say that no such mistaken idea existed in the church prior to the beginning of the biblical counseling movement in 1970 with the publication of Jay Adams' book *Competent to Counsel*.[1]

Jones admits to counseling Julie "with Nate" and "without Nate" (p. 259). As we explain in Chapter 5, this violates biblical restrictions to the contrary and should not be done. To Jones' credit, he does include two women who greatly minister to Julie, especially at critical times.

Jones says:

> Nate and our counseling team agreed that Julie needed to detoxify at an in-patient facility. Julie objected but eventually acquiesced. We found a recommended site in another state where she was admitted for 30 days. Our phone communication was limited during this time, but we were able to maintain minimal contact (p. 270).

Jones reveals that, while the "in-patient facility achieved its detoxifying goal" (p. 270), Julie committed adultery with one of the men during her stay. Since it is admitted that there were both "non-Christian male and female patients" (p. 271) at the facility, we conclude that it was a non-Christian facility, which was a poor choice.

The adultery could not have occurred at those Christian facilities of which we are aware.

Jones' discussion of Julie's sex life (pp. 271, 275, 279, 282, 283) was not necessary and was a violation of Ephesians 5:12 and the privacy of the marriage bed as we indicated earlier. However, the general conduct of Jones and others who counseled with him is biblically commendable.

Even though this case is a composite from other cases, Jones reveals some transparency that is little seen throughout *CTHC*. At one critical point Jones says, "I wish I could tell you that this counsel and plea turned Julie's heart. But it did not. Instead, things were about to worsen yet again" (p. 273). Later Jones reveals:

> On one of these occasions, Julie slid into an out-of-control mania that could not be overcome even by hours of biblical talk. All of our efforts to talk her down—face-to-face or by phone—were fruitless. On one occasion, from 12:45–1:30 in the morning we sat by the phone as I repeatedly sought (to no avail) to center her mind on Ps 121:1–2: "I lift my eyes toward the mountains. Where will my help come from? My help comes from the Lord, the Maker of heaven and earth" (p. 280).

At the end of the case Jones confesses:

> As I reflect on my relationship with Nate and Julie, I realize that I did a good job but not a great job. At times I should have intervened more quickly; early on I missed the depth of Julie's problems; **I could have probed more deeply into Julie's**

> **life and history**; I misunderstood her psychiatric medications and how the doctors were trying to treat her; I underestimated the strength of her addictions; and I failed to adapt my own counseling strategy with Julie quickly enough. While I **had used many of the same counseling methods successfully for many years, in Julie's case they didn't seem to "take."** Through this hard case God was not only gracious in changing Julie but was equally gracious in growing me into a more competent counselor (p. 285, bold added).

Contrary to what Jones says, he should **not** have probed "more deeply into Julie's life and history," as it is not necessary to even know her history in order to minister God's grace to her and let the Holy Spirit convict her and conform her life into the image of Christ, which would best be done through her husband or another woman.

At the beginning, Jones speaks of the Julie case occurring early in his ministry, which started when he was 26, but at the end he says he "had used many of the same counseling methods successfully for many years," but that "in Julie's case they didn't seem to 'take'" (p. 286). The time frame sounds a bit confused, but perhaps this is because of many cases over time having been molded together. While one may learn something about how Jones counsels women from this composite case, we question the biblical validity of doing so.

Case 10

"'Jennifer' and an Apparent Hard Case"

Considering that *CTHC* is touted as a book about the hard cases, it seems contradictory to include what may have appeared as "an Apparent Hard Case' at the beginning and then turns out **not** to be a "hard case" after all. Instead, it was a medical case having to do with a urinary tract infection and sleep deprivation, which can lead to symptoms of confusion and even paranoia. John Babler, PhD, says that, while this did not end up being a "hard case," it should be included so that others would not shy away from people with such initial symptoms. He then says, "Most wise Christians could be helpful with this kind of case if they took the time to listen well and fully understand what was actually taking place in the mind and heart of the person involved" (p. 287). But, how would one know whether or not this is a "hard case" or actually a medical problem rather than a counseling need?

Before getting into Babler's description of Jennifer, we must mention that those in the BCM honestly believe that if they get enough information (extensive data gathering) they will indeed be able, as Babler claims, to "fully understand what [is] actually taking place in the mind and heart of the person involved" (p. 287). This is highly presumptuous and reveals some self-deception on their part. While they may be able to put a few pieces together, the idea that they can "fully understand" anyone's "mind and heart" is incredible. No one can "fully understand" their own mind and heart, let alone another person's (Jer. 17:9). Only the Lord can know the mind and heart! The rest of us, including BCM counselors, have to settle for guessing. They may not feel as though they are guessing and missing the mark, because most counselees receive such analyses by looking for things inside them that match the counselor's words. After all, the counselor is the expert, so the needy counselee usually succumbs to almost any suggestion or diagnosis the counselor may make.

At the beginning of the case, Babler describes meeting Jennifer, "the wife of one of our students," who was "in the emergency room at a local hospital" (p. 288). Jennifer's husband, Jim, had noticed that "she had been acting strangely for several weeks and…she did not go to bed at all [the previous] Sunday night." In fact, Babler learned that Jennifer "had been having a difficult time sleeping for over a week." In addition, Babler said, "Jennifer experienced constant difficulty sleeping and told me she had not slept more than an hour a night for the last two weeks" (p. 288). Add to this the fact that Jennifer "had a urinary tract infection requiring an antibiotic" (p. 289). At the end of his case Babler says:

> The case of Jennifer and Jim reveals that sometimes bizarre and serious behavior can be a product of a combination of stressors, bad decisions, sleep deprivation, significant changes in life, and the ever-present challenge of spiritual warfare for the Christian (p. 299).

Add this all up and it results in questionable "challenging situations" (p. 299). Two synonyms for the word "apparent" as in an "Apparent Hard Case" are "visible" and "clear." So Jennifer is a visible or clear hard case, but that does not make any sense because Babler himself admits that this is not actually a "hard case" by describing all the preceding events and symptoms and says at the end, "Initially I considered this a hard counseling case" and then he proceeds to explain the following:

> Planning a wedding, finishing a challenging college degree, graduation, a wedding, an illness, a major move, and sleep deprivation would impact anyone. Once the emergency symptoms were dealt with, counseling proceeded in a way that any wise and growing Christian should be equipped to navigate (p. 299).

At no time did Babler refer to this as a "seemingly hard case."

We fault Babler, as we do the others, when he says, "Jennifer was given a clean bill of health" as the basis for proceeding. As we repeatedly emphasize, "A clean bill of health" does not mean that a person has "a clean bill of health" and that an illness may not be involved.

Several issues are related to our concerns about this case. First, Babler offers and then counsels a woman alone and then counsels Jim and Jennifer as a couple (see Chapter 3). Second, he offers to counsel her prior to speaking with her husband to obtain his permission. Third, he turns a doubly doubtful "Hard Case" into an "Apparent Hard Case," contrary to the evidence he provides. (See sleep disorders and sleep deprivation comments and footnotes in the case of "'Tony' and Bipolar Disorder.")

Note that Babler says, "When I met with Jennifer the next morning, she said she had slept for about 12 hours and was feeling a little better" (p. 289). He says of a later meeting with Jennifer, "There was no mention of her paranoia, and she remarked at least twice how much difference a little sleep made" (p. 292). Later yet, Babler says, "Jennifer admitted that she still remained anxious about things in their life together, but she was sleeping well. She no longer heard voices and did not feel as paranoid" (p. 294). With no further "hard case" sounding information the reader can see that this was not actually a hard case and should not have been referred to as such.

Babler heard that Jennifer's parents had become intrusive in Jim and Jennifer's lives after their wedding, which added to her stress. Although Jim "expressed willingness to meet with Jennifer and her father if it would be beneficial" (p. 293), it was Babler who actually met with Jennifer and her father. The talk about both Jim and Jennifer's parents was unnecessary and the role Babler plays with Jennifer's parents is characteristic of biblical counselors usurping the authority of the husband, as we mention in Chapter 5.

Another defect in Babler's counseling is his nosing into their sex life and showcasing it in his report. Babler's intervening in this area was unnecessary, especially since the problem was brought on by Jennifer's illness rather than some need for sex therapy. Babler says:

> In light of Jennifer's sickness during their honeymoon and the challenges thereafter, sexual intimacy had been nonexistent. As they focused on

these problem areas and ways to love and serve each other, God had been working to deepen their sex life as well (p. 298).

Actually once the bladder infection, which was probably a major cause of her lack of sleep as well as other disturbances, was over, Jim and Jennifer would have been able to have God "deepen their sex life" without Babler.

CTHC is not a book about mistaken hard cases, but is promoted as actually and literally about hard cases, which Babler's case of Jennifer is not. The editors made a mistake including Babler's case in a book about "hard cases." Using this case makes it seem as though the editors had a difficult time finding enough "hard cases" to include in their book.

7

"Concluding Reflections"

Much of what Lambert and Scott say in their "Concluding Reflections" is commendable regarding the sufficiency of Scripture and how believers can minister care and concern, guidance and compassion to one another in the Body of Christ. What they say about the power of Scripture and the power of Christ's love expressed through believers to those experiencing challenges in living does apply to all believers. They aptly quote from Galatians 6:1-2, 9-10 to show the need for believers to actively care for one another. Indeed, we are to carry one another's burdens, we are to listen compassionately, we are to minister hope, and we are to minister the Word of God as led by the Holy Spirit. **However, nobody in the church needs to be a counselor, particularly following mindlessly the methodology presented in *Counseling the Hard Cases* (*CTHC*), some of which would be contrary to Scripture and reflective of psychological counseling.**

What the biblical counseling movement has done is to formalize and systematize what should be a biblically based caring for one another in the local church. We have argued in the past that if God had needed psychotherapeutic systems and methodologies to minister to His people before the twentieth century, He would have included those theories and techniques in Scripture. Now we carry it a step further. If God had needed those methodologies of *CTHC* and the BCM that reflect psychological counseling theories and therapies, He would have included them in Scripture. Many of the specifics of what they do and how they do it are not all biblical. Too much has been recycled from psychological counseling.[1]

Lambert and Scott speak of two kinds of people who avoid doing counseling, which is an either/or fallacy: those who do not understand the sufficiency of Scripture and those who don't care enough to help (p. 303). We would add a third category and that would be those of us who believe in the sufficiency of Scripture to minister to problems of living and who care enough to become involved, but who eschew the rigid, authoritarian, one-up/one-down, certification-dependent methodology of biblical counseling that often reflects the problem-centered psychotherapeutic world in actual practice.

Lambert and Scott attempt to soften the authoritative and demeaning one-up position of the counselor by saying that:

> When we are seeking to minister to others in need, it actually is a mistake to think that the counselee is the only one in need. Actually, all of God's people in the counseling room are in need of growing in their faith in Christ. The Holy Spirit does not take a sabbatical on the counselor's sanctification while he or she is ministering

to others. Faithful counselors should regularly say after counseling, "Wow, I needed to hear what they said" or "I needed to hear what Scripture said" (p. 307).

We have read numerous counseling cases and descriptions but have never read such a statement following counseling as, "Wow, I needed to hear what they said." It certainly was not said at the end of either Lambert's or Scott's cases.

Lambert and Scott are of the opinion that all pastors are biblically mandated to be counseling their people in addition to preaching. Although there are instances of personal ministry in Scripture, preaching and teaching are highlighted as the primary means of communicating the Gospel and the new life in Christ. Aside from Christ and the apostles being able to heal miraculously, their personal ministry was one of teaching. There is no instance of a married couple airing their grievances week after week as in two of the cases mentioned earlier. Paul simply taught believers how married couples should treat one another, e.g., 1 Corinthians 7:3-4; Ephesians 5:23-33.

Rather than emphasizing counseling, the Scriptures emphasize teaching. For instance, Paul wrote to Timothy: "And the things that thou hast heard of me among many witnesses, the same commit thou to faithful men, who shall be able to teach others also" (2 Tim. 2:2). The older women were to teach the younger women: "To be discreet, chaste, keepers at home, good, obedient to their own husbands, that the word of God be not blasphemed" (Titus 2:5).

Every pastor should devote himself to praying, studying the Word, preaching, teaching, and equipping the saints, as they mature in the Word and the Spirit, to minister to each other as well as communicate the Gospel to others. A biblically based church with believers who have been well taught in the Word, lived accordingly, and have found the Lord faithful in small and great trials, will have sufficient resources to minister to the needs that arise. We have seen the Lord put people together for mutual care without any human assignment or imposed system. Sadly, however, people have learned, first from the world and then from the church, that they need experts in counseling, and so they may not seek help from "ordinary believers" unless they are trained and certified. Lambert and Scott, perhaps unknowingly, are promoting the myth of the superiority of the trained expert over the untrained ones who are living the Christian life and able to minister.

Erroneously, Lambert and Scott equate their kind of biblical counseling with the personal ministry people need. While their primary target is pastors, Lambert and Scott recommend that every believer become a biblical counselor, as they **"urge all Christians** toward the battlefield of love— the task of walking with broken people **in the work of counseling"** (p. 305, bold added). However, that would be very restrictive. Instead of following Scripture and the work of the Holy Spirit in their lives, the pastors especially, along with all members of a congregation, would have to learn the techniques and methodologies of data gathering, delving into the past to hear unconfirmed stories (Prov. 18:13 misused), probing for more details (Eph. 5:12 abused), enabling and encouraging gossip, complaining (murmuring), and other forms of sinful communication, and confronting any sin in the counselee that may appear or even be suspected, such as unseen "idols of the heart."

Lambert and Scott speak of the "hard work of loving people through counseling." How much does a counselor love every client, particularly if the client is paying? Lambert is a great promoter of David Powlison, who is listed as the first endorser of *CTHC* and who is head of the Christian Counseling and Educational Foundation (CCEF), where counselees are charged fees for counseling. Lambert heads the Association of Certified Biblical Counselors (ACBC), which includes some certificated members who charge fees and a board member who charges fees as well. To our knowledge neither Lambert nor Scott have publicly exposed the great unbiblical error of charging. Can one purchase love through buying into biblical counseling?

Love can more freely be expressed in a body of believers who grasp the truth about the sufficiency of God's Word, the indwelling work of the Holy Spirit, and the love of God, **but who are not hampered by a rigid counseling format or requirements for specialized BCM training, credentials, or certificates**. True ministry to one another is an act of love and we believe that many biblical counselors do love their clients. However, the structure of the counseling puts one believer above another in a one-up position. One-up is the counselor who diagnoses the spiritual problem, prescribes the homework, issues orders,[2] and confronts major or minor sins of the one-down counselee, which may or may not be apparent. Here the counselor may assume too much spiritual authority, as Lambert did in the case of Sarah and Clark, rather than simply teaching the authoritative Word regarding what may appear applicable and then trusting the Holy Spirit to make the direct application and conviction of sin, without usurping the husband's headship or lording it over the wife.

Even within the description of *CTHC* one can see how counselees are sometimes demeaned rather than treated as equal at the foot of the cross. What would it be like to be in a church where everyone is busy counseling one another according to the BCM methodology? Not only would this fictionalize fellowship; it would displace the work of the Holy Spirit to convict according to His work in believers as they respond to preaching and teaching. Such an environment would be spiritually stifling! Thankfully, Christ did not include "counselor" in His ministry gifts to the church in Ephesians 4:11ff. Instead He sent the Holy Spirit to be our perpetual guide, who does not have to guess and presume, but who knows all things about every individual!

We have given evidence that the word *counseling* is not in Scripture and that there are problems with how those in the BCM use the words *counsel* and *counselor*.[3] They fail to see that the practice of biblical counseling as it is done today is not in Scripture. Moreover, Lambert equates ministry with counseling and counseling with ministry, as if the two are the same, in his book *The Biblical Counseling Movement after Adams*:

> This is not a book about counseling. Even though you might be tempted to think it is a book about counseling, it is really a book about ministry. The

fact is that counseling is ministry, and ministry is counseling. The two are equivalent terms.[4]

Making *counseling* and *ministry* equivalent terms goes against language and logic. Such a statement reminds us of William Kroger's expanded definition of *hypnosis* in his talk titled "No Matter How You Slice It, It's Hypnosis." Kroger even turns daily conversations into hypnosis.[5] To show how ridiculous Lambert's statement equating ministry and counseling is, perhaps one might say, "No matter how you slice it, all ministry is counseling and all counseling is ministry."

Ministry is not counseling as in the BCM and counseling as in the BCM is not ministry, though it may include ministry of the Word. Whether you look into the history and tradition of the church or the Bible itself, biblical counseling as practiced by the BCM does not exist and it did not exist. It is a recent phenomenon in the church, which some in the BCM readily admit. The way BCM counseling is conducted is more reflective of the psychological movement that preceded it and is definitely NOT ministry. Although counseling may include personal ministry, the ministry of the Word through the Holy Spirit in the fellowship of the saints cannot and should never be reduced to counseling, particularly the problem-centered counseling practiced in the BCM and promulgated by Lambert, Scott, et al. in *CTHC*.

Lambert and Scott cite a number of verses to make it look as if these justify and describe their form of counseling. They evidently think that Paul was counseling as done in the BCM as he taught "publickly, and from house to house" (Acts 20:20). **Paul was teaching, not counseling!** While he may have been giving godly advice and wise counsel, he was not counseling in the manner practiced today. Teaching and counseling are not equivalent, though counseling may include some teaching and teaching may include wise counsel. Paul taught and expected the Holy Spirit to make the personal applications. Lambert and Scott also use Galatians 6:1-2 as if brethren coming alongside a brother "overtaken in a fault" are examples of today's BCM counseling. The qualification for one to come alongside was to be spiritual (walking according to the Spirit), not qualified through any form of certification or training aside from their own knowledge of Scripture and walk with the Lord. Lambert and Scott add Galatians 6:9-10 to verses 1 and 2 and say, "The word *counseling* never appears in this text, but the passage is all about counseling as it is understood in contemporary culture" (p. 303). The text is not "about counseling as it is understood in contemporary culture." Contemporary counseling in a contemporary culture is a contradiction to the original meaning of Galatians 6:1-2, 9-10. It is simply an example of how one can misuse Scripture to make it fit contemporary thinking and practices.

Unlike admonitions and examples from Scripture, BCM counselors are in the business of data gathering, diagnosing, treating, and solving problems, much like their psychological predecessors. Their strong point is teaching Scripture during counseling sessions, but too much time is spent airing grievances, prying for details from the past and present, and story-telling gossip. One wonders how much disobedience to the Word regarding murmuring is stimulated by the intense data gathering, much of which ends up as just plain grousing about other people and circumstances. One does not have to be trained in biblical counseling to follow the Scriptures that Lambert and Scott put forth, such as "Now we exhort you, brethren, warn them that are unruly, comfort the feebleminded, support the weak, be patient toward all men." Notice that this admonition is addressed to the "brethren" (i. e., fellow believers), not specially trained, certificated counselors. All believers need to be prayerful and careful about confronting fellow believers, because we do not know the order God is following in His sanctifying work in any individual. We all have many faults and God may have a different order of conviction and change than those things that may be obvious to a counselor. Moreover, the need for patience with one another in the local church does not come from sitting in classes about how to counsel. Instead, patience is the gracious work of the Holy Spirit in a child of God often developed through trials (Rom. 5:1-5).

In their encouragement for pastors and parishioners to minister to troubled believers, Lambert and Scott are actually discouraging the ministry of mutual care in the Body of Christ with their methodology and emphasis on credentials. Their love of credentials can be seen in the name change from NANC (National Association of Nouthetic Counselors) to ACBC (Association of Certified Biblical Counselors) with the significant addition of *Certified*. Not only must one be **certified**, but there are levels of **certification, with some more certified than others**. Considering that both Lambert and Scott are professors of biblical counseling at a seminary and that Lambert is the Executive Director of ACBC, their encouragement for everyone in the church to be a biblical counselor would match who they are professionally and would dramatically increase the demand for their services. We agree that all believers should become knowledgeable of the Word, be growing in the things of Spirit, and be actively loving one another with the compassion of the Lord to care for one another as needs arise. We describe what to avoid and what can be done in our books *Person to Person Ministry* and *Stop Counseling! Start Ministering!*[6]

We conclude by repeating our **WARNING: Do not blithely and blindly play follow-the-leader with the ten case studies showcased in *CTHC*. Do not take literally these ten cases and the inferred claim that you, too, can cure[7] through biblical counseling the hard cases listed in *CTHC* plus, by extension, the other 300 mental disorders[8] listed in the *Diagnostic and Statistical Manual of Mental Disorders* (*DSM*) that do not have medical markers and where no organic issues are found after a full medical workup!**

Appendix

Counselor, Counselee, Counseling

Old Testament *Counsel*

In the Old Testament there are just five English words (translated from a number of Hebrew words) that seem to relate to the currently used term *counseling*. They are *counsel, counselled, counsellor, counsellors*, and *counsels*.[1] The words translated as *counsellor* and *counsellors* are used in reference to the person giving the counsel. The other ones have to do with what is counseled.

There are at least two ways to examine these words: in their original meaning and in their context. The most frequently used word, *counsel*, and its derivatives can be translated as "advise, counsel, purpose, devise, plan."[2] The repeated usage of the word *counsel* (124 times in the Old Testament) is for decision making or to accomplish a goal. For instance, when Absalom conspired to take the kingdom away from his father and sought counsel, Ahithophel proposed a plan to pursue David, smite him, and then bring those who had followed David back to Absalom. However, when Absalom consulted Hushai about the plan, Hushai said, "The counsel that Ahithophel hath given is not good at this time." Hushai then proposed another plan by which Absalom, instead, would be defeated (2 Samuel 17).

Counsel had to do with plans, guidance, and advice. Psalm 1:1 says, "Blessed is the man that walketh not in the counsel of the ungodly." That is, do not follow the advice, guidance, or plans of the ungodly. Psalm 2:2 gives another example of counsel: "The kings of the earth set themselves, and the rulers take counsel together, against the Lord, and against his anointed." Here a group is devising a plan in opposition to God.

If one compares the actual, contextual use of the word *counsel*, as well as the words *counsels* and *counselled*, one will see a great contrast between the biblical use of those words and the way current biblical counselors counsel counselees in their personal, marital, and family problems of living. While there may be times when biblical counselors devise plans, propose a course of action, and give advice, the current practice of biblical counseling contains elements that go way beyond the biblical use of the word *counsel*.

One often misused example to establish biblical counseling is found in Exodus 18:13-26. The passage begins with a picture of Moses as he "sat to judge the people" and as "the people stood by Moses from the morning unto the evening." Moses' father-in-law, Jethro, asked Moses why that was happening and Moses answered:

> Because the people come unto me to inquire of God: When they have a matter, they come unto me; and I judge between one and another, and I do make them know the statutes of God, and his laws (Ex. 18:15-16).

In other words, Moses was judging according to the law of God. The word *counsel* is not even used to describe what Moses was doing. The word *counsel* is not used until Jethro is ready to give advice and present a plan to Moses, when Jethro said to Moses: "Hearken now unto my voice, I will give thee counsel." Jethro then presented a plan for Moses to teach the ordinances of God to the people and to:

> ... provide out of all the people able men, such as fear God, men of truth, hating covetousness; and place such over them, to be rulers of thousands, and rulers of hundreds, rulers of fifties, and rulers of tens: And let them judge the people at all seasons: and it shall be, that every great matter they shall bring unto thee, but every small matter they shall judge: so shall it be easier for thyself, and they shall bear the burden with thee (Exodus 18:21,22).

One commentary says the following about Moses:

> Having been employed to redeem Israel out of the house of bondage, herein he is a further type of Christ, that he is employed as a lawgiver and a judge among them. (1) He was to answer enquiries, and to explain the laws of God that were already given them, concerning the Sabbath, the manna, &c., beside the laws of nature, relating both to piety and equity, *v* 15. Moses made them *know the statutes of God and his laws, v.* 16. His business was, not to make laws, but to make known God's laws; his place was but that of a servant. (2) He was to decide controversies, judging between a man and his fellow, *v* 16. And,

if the people were as quarrelsome one with another as they were with God, no doubt he had a
great many causes brought before him.[3]

It must also be remembered that this incident preceded Mt. Sinai and the receiving of the Ten Command-
ments. Moses was judging the people. He was resolv-
ing controversies when disagreements occurred. **He was
not counseling problems of living like a contemporary biblical counselor but was judging according to
the law of God.** While judging according to the Word
of God may be included in biblical counseling, there is
a great difference between what Moses was doing and
what present-day biblical counselors generally do.

In their eagerness to justify what they do, those who
refer to themselves as "biblical counselors" turn judges
into counselors who follow a pattern that more resembles psychological counseling than judging by God's
laws and ordinances. Many years ago, in our own eagerness for counseling according to the Word of God, we
used Jethro's counsel to Moses to encourage pastors to
share the burden of personal counsel with members of
the body. We continue to believe that the principle of
sharing the burden applies, but we now conclude that the
story of Jethro's advice to Moses is misapplied as a justification for the methodology of what is currently called
"biblical counseling."

Another verse misused is Proverbs 11:14: "Where no
counsel is the people fall; but in the multitude of counsellors there is safety." The word *people* is defined as "a
people (as a congregated *unit*); spec. a *tribe* (as those of
Israel); hence (collect.) *troops* or *attendants*; fig. a flock:
—folk, men nation, people."[4] The *multitude* refers to a

great number and not just one person. So, in no way can this verse be used to justify contemporary counseling.

Counselors in the church also use Isaiah 9:6 to justify their practice of counseling:

> For unto us a child is born, unto us a son is given: and the government shall be upon his shoulder: and his name shall be called Wonderful, Counsellor, The mighty God, The everlasting Father, The Prince of Peace (Isaiah 9:6).

Isaiah 9:6 prophetically describes the coming Messiah, the Lord Jesus Christ. In this passage Jesus is called "Wonderful, Counsellor." The authorized King James Version separates the words *wonderful* from *counselor* with a comma, but Hebrew scholars say that the word *wonderful* is used to describe *counselor*. Therefore we looked into the meaning of both words. The word *wonderful* is the translation of the Hebrew word *pele'*. The *Theological Wordbook of the Old Testament* defines the Hebrew word *pele'* as "wonder" and says that it is: "Always in a context of God's acts or words, except for Lam 1:9. The root appears most frequently in the Psalms."[5] Thus it has to do with the wonder of the miraculous. It is beyond the common meaning of *wonderful* in English.

The word *counselor* (KJV) is from the Hebrew word *yâ'ats*, which means "advise, counsel, purpose, devise, plan," and is translated by a word from the Greek *boule* family (word group) in the Septuagint (the Greek translation of the Old Testament). Jesus as counselor is unique in that He is the very Word of God who "was made flesh, and dwelt among us" (John 1:14). He did not practice counseling as those who call themselves "biblical counselors" today. There were no ongoing sessions centered around individual people's problems. He knew the heart and spoke forth the Word of Truth. Today we receive His counsel through the written Word together with the Holy Spirit. The involvement of the Holy Spirit in the Lord's counsel can be seen in Isaiah 11:1-2:

> And there shall come forth a rod out of the stem of Jesse, and a Branch shall grow out of his roots: And the spirit of the LORD shall rest upon him, the spirit of wisdom and understanding, the spirit of counsel and might, the spirit of knowledge and of the fear of the LORD.

Jesus is the Branch, and the word translated *counsel* comes from a derivative of the same Hebrew word as translated *counsellor* in Isaiah 9:6. The connection is clearly seen between the Wonderful Counselor and the "spirit of counsel." Therefore, this Hebrew word group cannot be used to justify the kind of counseling that goes on in *Counseling the Hard Cases* (*CTHC*), as well as in the BCM. Nevertheless, we can be confident that God will continue to give counsel through His Word and His Holy Spirit. That is why solid Bible preaching, teaching, and evangelizing are so vital today and must be an integral part of ministering to individuals, couples, and families in need.

New Testament *Counsel*

The words *counseled* and *counselors* are found only in the Old Testament. In the New Testament, there are only three words used in translation that seem to relate to the currently used terms in counseling. They are *counsel, counsellor,* and *counsels.* One of these words (*counsellor*) has to do with the person or persons giving the counsel. The remaining two have to do with what is counseled.

The English word *counsel* is used 19 times in the New Testament (KJV, *Strong's Concordance*[6]) and each comes from the Greek *boule* word group, which means purpose, will, decision, resolution, counsel, or advice. If one looks under the word *counsel* in a concordance and then reads this New Testament word in the context of the verses listed, it will hardly be necessary to look in the Greek dictionary to understand the meaning.

In many instances the word *counsel* is used to describe the actions of those who opposed Jesus and His disciples. For instance, Matthew 27:1 says, "When the morning was come, all the chief priests and elders of the people took counsel together against Jesus to put him to death." The word translated *counsel* in that and similar passages refers to the idea of consulting together.

In contrast to the wicked counsel engaged in by the enemies of Christ is the counsel of God, such as in Ephesians 1:11, which speaks of believers "being predestinated according to the purpose of him who worketh all things after the counsel of his own will." The same word is used in Acts 20:27, when Paul says, "For I have not shunned to declare unto you all the counsel of God." Indeed some biblical counselors will declare much counsel of God in the process of their counseling, and that is what should go on in ministries among believers. Yet, again, that is only part of what occurs in contemporary biblical counseling. **The contemporary use of *counsel* in reference to biblical counseling relates only distantly and tangentially to the meanings of the words used in the New Testament.**

The word *counsellor* is used only three times in the New Testament. Two of the times are used to describe Joseph of Arimathaea and refer to his position as a member of the Jewish Sanhedrin (Mark 15:43; Luke 23:15). The other verse is Romans 11:34: "For who hath known the mind of the Lord? or who hath been his counsellor?" In other words, who would be so arrogant as to think he could advise God? None of these verses in the New Testament can rightly be used as a justification for the contemporary term *counselor* nor can they be used to support such a person. **There is no example of biblical counseling as it is practiced in the church today.**

However, one of the root meanings of the Greek words *sumboulos* and *bouleutes* translated *counsellor* or *counselor* is "adviser." If contemporary counselors, such as those in the BCM, functioned only as in the Bible, a person or couple would come seeking advice. The advice would be given and that would be the end of it, rather than numerous sessions filled with much talk and many probing questions about the "counselee's" problems regarding past and present relationships, circumstances, and feelings, as one finds throughout *CTHC*.

The only other word used is *counsels*, which is used only once, in 1 Corinthians 4:5: "Therefore judge nothing before the time, until the Lord come, who both will bring to light the hidden things of darkness, and will make manifest the counsels of the hearts: and then shall every man have praise of God." It is simply the plural of *boule*, which means purpose, will, decision, resolution, counsel, or advice. In this context *counsels* would refer to inner advising, planning, and directing within the heart of man.

Obviously the New Testament use of the words translated as *counsel, counsellor,* and *counsels* do have shades of meaning in the Greek. However, in no instance does the use of those words justify what is currently called "biblical counseling" in the twenty-first century. We are not saying that these are the only words and examples associated with counseling in the Old and New Testaments. **What we are saying is that there is no counseling with its roles of counselor and counselee found in the Bible as presently conducted by those who call themselves biblical counselors and in *CTHC*.** One cannot use the biblical meaning of the above words to defend the practice of contemporary biblical counseling. These terms have been usurped from secular use, retrofitted to Scripture, and then rationalized to be biblical.

Counselee and *Counseling*

Neither the Old nor the New Testament has an equivalent for the word *counselee*. In fact, the word *counselee* did not show up in a dictionary until 1934, when it was defined in the *Oxford English Dictionary* as "One who receives professional counselling." No wonder it is nowhere in the Bible. Psychological counseling created the need for a word to designate those receiving "professional counseling." Yet biblical counselors consistently call their recipients "counselees." The word *counselee(s)* is used prolifically in *CTHC* (83 times).

We discuss the biblical meanings and use of the biblical equivalents to the words *counselor* and *counseling* and conclude that **there is no word *counseling* or its equivalent found in the entire Bible and there was no practice of counseling as it is presently conducted by**

those counselors of the ten cases in *CTHC* and others who call themselves biblical counselors.[7] It is misleading to use biblical words and give them a new meaning to defend the practice of contemporary biblical counseling. Just because some of the words are the same does not mean that today's biblical counselors are doing the same thing as recorded in Scripture. Same words do not equal the same practice. If the activities are called "biblical counseling," then the words and activities should be biblical. To use words from Scripture in a way that those words are not used in Scripture is confusing at least and deceptive at worst. This is compounded by biblically rationalizing the activity of contemporary problem-centered biblical counseling where no such biblical examples exist. However, the word *counseling* is repeatedly used throughout *CTHC* to describe what they do.

Dr. Jay Adams' Use of the Words *Counsel* and *Counseling*

One of the rationalizations given by Adams for using the term *counsel* is as follows:

> Because the New Testament term [*noutheteo*] is larger than the English word "counsel," and because it doesn't carry any of the "freight" that is attached to the latter term, we have simply imported the biblical term into English.[8]

In his article "What Is Biblical Counseling?" Adams uses the following four verses from the Bible to describe his methodology and practice of counseling. He translates *noutheteo* uniquely here and in his own translation of the New Testament, titled *The Christian Counselor's*

New Testament,[9] with the words *counsel* and *counseling,* to apply these words to his system of counseling:

> Romans 15:14: "I myself am convinced about you, my brothers, that you yourselves are full of goodness, filled with all knowledge, and competent to **counsel** one another."

> 1 Thessalonians 5:12: "Now we ask you, brothers, to recognize those who labor among you, and manage you in the Lord, and **counsel** you."

> 1 Corinthians 4:14: "I am not writing these things to shame you, but to **counsel** you as my dear children."

> Acts 20:31: "Therefore, be alert, remembering that for three years, night and day, I didn't stop **counseling** each one of you with tears."

Adams says that the Greek verb *noutheteo* and noun *nouthesia* are "sometimes translated 'admonish, correct or instruct.'" Nevertheless, he **uniquely** chooses to translate these words as *counsel* and *counseling*. While some versions translate the Greek verb as *warn,* **we found no other version that translated *noutheteo* and *nouthesia* as *counsel* and *counseling.*** We checked these four verses with numerous versions of the English Bible, excluding amplified and paraphrased versions, and **found no support for Adams' translation of these Greek words as *counsel* and *counseling*.** We also used an expository dictionary and a Greek-English lexicon and again **found no support for Adams' translation using the words *counsel* and *counseling*.**[10]

The word *counsel* as used by both psychological and biblical counselors is loaded with all kinds of notions about people and various methods of helping people change. Moreover, no word translated as *counsel* in the Bible ever meant anything close to what goes on in present-day counseling where two or three people meet to talk about one person's or one couple's problems, complaints, feelings, and behavior week after week, where the focus of the conversation is the *counselee* (newly created word for the recipient of professional counseling during the 20th century) and the counselee's problems.

Adams also translates the following passages with *counsel* or a derivative:

> *noutheteo* as *counseling* in Acts 20:31; Col. 1:28;

> *noutheteo* as *counsel* Romans 15:14; 1 Cor. 4:14; Col. 3:16; 1 Thes. 5: 12,14; 2 Thes. 3:15;

> *nouthesia* as *counseling* in Titus 3:10.

Adams says, "The three ideas found in the word *nouthesia* are **Confrontation**, **Concern**, and **Change**"[11] (emphasis his). However, **none of those words can be found as translations of the word *nouthesia* in the numerous versions of the Bible we checked. While Adams' form of counseling may include admonishment, correction, and instruction at times, there is also a great deal more that goes on, including many unbiblical practices.**[12]

The words *counsel* and *counseling* in the BCM, as we have just indicated, resemble secular counseling and not what Jesus and Paul did. We think it more accurate to say that the words *noutheteo* and *nouthesia* were hijacked from the New Testament and transformed into *counsel* and *counseling* to give a biblical

justification for what those who call themselves "biblical counselors" do and to avoid the obvious relationship to secular counseling with the "freight" that accompanies it.

In the Old Testament the word *counsel* is used 124 times and in the New Testament it is used 19 times. Thus in the entire Bible the word *counsel* is used 143 times. Nevertheless, Jay Adams does not quote one of these verses to justify his counseling methodology in his book *Competent to Counsel*. Without quoting the verses, he does refer to three of them.

New Testament Gifts and Callings

Because of the priesthood of all believers in the body of Christ (1 Pet. 2:9), all are to serve and minister to spiritual and physical needs of one another as each is called and gifted by the Holy Spirit for ministry (Rom. 12:8). This includes ministering the Word, encouraging, exhorting, helping, and teaching, but all from a position of humility. While some believers are called and ordained to specific positions of ministry, such as elders, deacons, pastors and teachers, all may minister and serve one another as the Holy Spirit equips and leads. In every conversation believers are to be speaking what is "good to the use of edifying, that it may minister grace unto the hearers" (Eph. 4:29). Edifying conversation among believers is indeed ministry. Therefore, *ministering* is both a far better word and activity among believers than *counseling* as prolifically used in *CTHC*.

Where is the office of counselor in the New Testament? Is there a specific calling of counselor as there is for evangelists, pastors and teachers? Are there specific offices for a counselor as there are for elders and deacons? Why is the position of counselor absent, for instance, in Ephesians 4, which speaks of Christ's gifts to the church:

> And he gave some, apostles; and some, prophets; and some, evangelists; and some, pastors and teachers; for the perfecting of the saints, for the work of the ministry, for the edifying of the body of Christ: Till we all come in the unity of the faith, and of the knowledge of the Son of God, unto a perfect man, unto the measure of the stature of the fulness of Christ (Eph. 4:11-13).

Romans 12:4-13 describes the function of the Body of Christ with members using their spiritual gifts for the spiritual benefit of one another:

> For as we have many members in one body, and all members have not the same office: So we, being many, are one body in Christ, and every one members one of another. Having then gifts differing according to the grace that is given to us (vv. 4-6a).

Note all that is accomplished through these gifts of ministry described throughout these passages. The great emphasis on counseling today is amazing in that "counselor" is not in the list. Through all the gifts of ministry, along with the Word of God and the Holy Spirit, the saints would be perfected, that is, become mature in the faith. They would be equipped to do the "work of the ministry," they would be built up, they would come to unity based on their common faith in the Lord Jesus Christ, and they would increase in their knowledge of

Christ. Moreover, through those gifts of ministry, they would be so established in truth that they would not be deceived (Eph. 4:14).

Besides the gifts of ministry, there is the Body of Christ "fitly joined together and compacted by that which every joint supplieth, according to the effectual working in the measure of every part, maketh increase of the body unto the edifying of itself in love" (Eph. 4:16). Here is where the one-to-one ministry occurs: the one-another edifying, encouraging, and supplying what is needed—the mutual caring, giving, and loving—occurring as naturally as the different parts of the human body work together for health and well-being. There is no one-up/one-down relationship of counselor and counselee. Instead there is the mutual care, encouragement, and edification of all members of the Body of Christ. Counsel may be given and received, but **it is the Holy Spirit**, who indwells every believer, who sees into the inner man, who applies the Word and makes it effectual in the believer, and then who enables the believer to glorify God through love and obedience, as most clearly taught in Romans 8:26-27:

> Likewise the Spirit also helpeth our infirmities: for we know not what we should pray for as we ought: but the Spirit itself maketh intercession for us with groanings which cannot be uttered. And he that searcheth the hearts knoweth what is the mind of the Spirit, because he maketh intercession for the saints according to the will of God.

It has been said by some, and we agree, that those who take the position of counselor in someone else's life may be usurping the role of the Holy Spirit at times.

Believers are called to comfort (1 Thess. 5:11), instruct (2 Tim. 2:24-26), edify (Rom. 14:19), admonish (Rom. 15:14), forgive (Eph. 4:32), and restore (Gal. 6:1) one another. However, the only one who can accurately see inside a person and therefore be the real counselor is the Lord Himself.

Rather than emphasizing counseling, the Scriptures emphasize teaching. For instance, Paul wrote to Timothy: "And the things that thou hast heard of me among many witnesses, the same commit thou to faithful men, who shall be able to teach others also" (2 Tim. 2:2). The older women were to teach the younger women: "To be discreet, chaste, keepers at home, good, obedient to their own husbands, that the word of God be not blasphemed" (Titus 2:5).

Some biblical counselors claim that they are simply teachers or that they are simply discipling other believers. If that is the case, why do they call themselves "counselors" and why do they follow the format of worldly counseling? While we see instances of teaching in Scripture, such instances do not resemble the process of counseling as it is practiced today, with weekly problem-centered appointments.

The word translated *teachers* is *didaskalos*. If teaching is what they do, why not call it "biblical teaching" instead of "biblical counseling"? By picking up the word *counselor*, the rest of the baggage comes along. And, counseling is a big attraction. That's where the prestige is in Christendom today. Counselors are often held in higher regard than pastors, both inside and outside the church. The desire is for an expert in understanding human problems and how to deal with them. **The assump-**

tion is that the trained counselor has special knowledge. The unspoken implication is that the pastor does not, unless he is trained in counseling.

The special knowledge people seem to be looking for has to do with the soul itself, rather than external behavior. Among the biblical counselors there are those who counsel behavioristically and those who counsel analytically as they attempt to identify the idols of the heart. There are those who look for the answers to people's problems in their past and in their "unconscious." Some have attempted to control the field through certificates, diplomas, degrees, and organizations. However, there is no universal model or method of biblical counseling. **Each counselor uses the Bible according to some combination of personal experience, secular theories, biblical doctrines, and "common sense," as is done in** *CTHC.* **The common thread among them all is their problem centeredness.**

While those who call themselves "biblical counselors" may be operating according to Scripture to some degree, they do so **not** within a position delineated in Scripture, because the New Testament does not present the position of the contemporary counselor. If they do minister biblically to another believer, they do so simply as fellow believers or within ordained ministries presented in Scripture. **The replacement for psychological counseling is not biblical counseling. It is ministering the Word of God to one another in love, patience, and forbearance.** It involves believers being equipped through the gifts of ministry.

Our society places great value on the position of counselor. If the common name for a biblical counselor were "advisor" or "teacher" and the activity were called "advising" or "teaching," those would probably be the very words adopted by the church. Instead of "biblical counselors," there would be "biblical advisors" doing "biblical advising" or "biblical teachers" doing "biblical teaching." If those terms sound dull and flat, it's because the powerful cultural symbol is *counselor*, not *advisor* or *teacher*. An example of the centrality of biblical counseling over and above normal pastoral practice can be seen in the name change from *The Journal of Pastoral Practice* to *The Journal of Biblical Counseling*.

***Counselor*, *counselee*, and *counseling* are words that have been empowered and given status by a secular therapeutic society and adopted by the biblical counseling movement. These three terms are imbedded in the fabric of the secular society and provide a façade of culturally sanctioned assets to the biblical counseling movement. They give an air of "professionalism" to the practice of biblical counseling.**

Christians need to move away from using the designations "biblical counseling" and "biblical counselor." The words *counseling* and *counselor* have become powerful symbols and suffer the same shortcomings within the church as they do outside the church. Because the terms *counsel* (verb form), *counselor*, *counselee*, and *counseling* have such strong roots, meanings, "freight" (Adams), and ties to psychotherapy with no biblical basis for their use in ministry, we suggest replacing them with the following:

> *Counsel*: minister, evangelize, teach, pastor, disciple, come alongside, advise, encourage, admonish, exhort;

Counselor: minister, evangelist, teacher, pastor, fellow believer, helper, elder, brother, sister, the one who ministers;

Counselee: fellow believer, brother, sister (or, if not a believer, a possible convert), person, individual;

Counseling: ministering, pastoring, evangelizing, teaching, encouraging, exhorting, admonishing, advising.

One should not follow the example in *CTHC* in their use of the unbiblical words and practices of *counselor*, *counselee*, *counseling*, but rather use one or more of the above terms. **While some of these terms are not in Scripture, at least they are not contaminated by association with the psychological counseling movement and are in harmony with what Scripture teaches.**

Christ-centered ministry focuses on building one's faith through truth to encourage the troubled individual to grow spiritually, mature in the faith, and deal with his/her own problems as others do in relationship with the Lord. When one compares how Jesus and Paul ministered with the way those in the BCM counsel, there is a dramatic difference. While they may do some similar things as Jesus and Paul did, those in the BCM counsel more like secular counselors than like Jesus and Paul.

End Notes

Chapter 1: A Critical Review

1   Stuart Scott and Heath Lambert, eds. *Counseling the Hard Cases: True Stories Illustrating the Sufficiency of God's Resources in Scripture*. Nashville, TN: B&H Publishing Group, 2012, p. 301. Hereafter page references to this book will be in parentheses within the text.

2   Martin and Deidre Bobgan. *Person to Person Ministry: Soul Care in the Body of Christ*, Santa Barbara, CA: EastGate Publishers , 2009; *Stop Counseling! Start Ministering!* Santa Barbara, CA: EastGate Publishers, 2011.

3   David Powlison, "Cure of Souls (and the Modern Psychotherapies)," www.ccef. org/cure-souls-and-modern-psychotherapies.

4   Martin and Deidre Bobgan. *Against "Biblical Counseling": For the Bible*. Santa Barbara, CA: EastGate Publishers, 1994, Chapter 7, pp. 73-92.

5   Martin and Deidre Bobgan. *Christ-Centered Ministry versus Problem-Centered Counseling*. Santa Barbara, CA: EastGate Publishers. 2004; *Person to Person Ministry. op. cit.*; *Stop Counseling! Start Ministering! op. cit.*; *Against "Biblical Counseling": For the Bible, op. cit.*

6   Martin and Deidre Bobgan. *Person to Person Ministry, op. cit.*, chapters 3, 4, 29, 35.

7   Heath Lambert. *The Biblical Counseling Movement After Adams*. Wheaton, IL: Crossway, 2012, p. 46.

8   *Ibid.*, p. 47.

9   *Jay* E. Adams, "About this book…," *PsychoHeresy: The Psychological Seduction of Christianity*, Santa Barbara, CA: EastGate Publishers, 1987, endorsements page.

10 Jay E. Adams. *Grist from Adams' Mill*. Phillipsburg, NJ: Presbyterian and Reformed Publishing Co., 1983, p. 69.

11 We will **not** repeatedly use quotes around the word *biblical* when used with the words *counseling* and *counselor*, but let it be understood that, as we demonstrate in our past writing, biblical counseling is not biblical because it is sinfully problem-centered like the psychological counseling movement. Also, to avoid confusion we will use their (biblical counseling movement) terms of **counselor, counseling**, and **counselee**, even though there is no biblical support or justification for the use of such terms as we have demonstrated in our books *Against "Biblical Counseling": For the Bible*, Chapter 3, and *Person to Person Ministry*, Chapter 5.

12 We use the word *cure* throughout. Lambert prefers the term *heal*, as he has a series of blogs titled "Can Jesus Heal Mental Illness?" In J.I. Rodale's *The Synonym Finder*, *cure* is the first synonym for *heal* and *curing* is the first synonym for *healing*.

13 We will be using the term *mental disorders* to stand for mental-emotional-behavioral disorders, sometimes referred to as *mental illness*, with the understanding that the word *mental* is used metaphorically. The mind itself is not a biological organ and therefore cannot be literally ill, but the symptoms may be mental, emotional, and/or behavioral.

14 Harvard Medical School *Mental Health Letter*, Vol. 2, No. 12, p. 1

15 E. Fuller Torrey. *Surviving Schizophrenia*, 5th Ed. New York: Harper. 2006. p. 156.

16 E. Fuller Torrey, email, 9/13/12.

17 Elyse Fitzpatrick and Laura Hendrickson. *Will Medicine Stop the Pain?* Chicago: Moody Publishers, 2006, p.175.

18 "A psychoactive drug, psychopharmaceutical, or psychotropic is a chemical substance that crosses the blood-brain barrier and acts primarily upon the central nervous system where it affects brain function, resulting in alterations in perception, mood, consciousness, cognition and behavior," en.wikipedia.org/wiki/Psychoactive_drug.

19 "Peter Breggin," en.wikipedia.org/wiki/Peter_Breggin, 8/24/2014.

20 Peter. R. Breggin. *Toxic Psychiatry*. New York: St. Martin's Press, 1991.

21 Hendrickson, *op. cit.*, back cover.

22 Martin and Deidre Bobgan, "Review of *Will Medicine Stop the Pain?*" *PsychoHeresy Awareness Letter*, 2009, Vol. 19, No. 5.

23 Hendrickson, *op. cit.*, p. 14.

24 "*DSM-5*: Psychiatrists' 'Bible' Finally Unveiled," *Huffington Post*, 5/16/2013, www.huffingtonpost.com.

Chapter 2: Cases, Anecdotes, and Science

1   The terms *counselor, counselee, counseling* are their terms. We have expressed our concern over the validity of using these in a Christian setting in our writings, including our books: *Against "Biblical Counseling": For the Bible*, Santa Barbara, CA: EastGate Publishers, 1994, pp. 57-72; *Person to Person Ministry: Soul Care in the Body of Christ*, Santa Barbara, CA: EastGate Publishers , 2009, pp. 42-51.

2   This section will use excerpts and paraphrases from our many past writings, including our book *Person to Person Ministry, op. cit.*, pp. 82-85.

3   Martin and Deidre Bobgan. *Stop Counseling! Start Ministering!* Santa Barbara, CA: EastGate Publishers, 2011, Chapter 3, pp. 71-5; *Person to Person Ministry, op. cit.*, pp. 92-114, 129-142; "A Critical Review of the Master's College & Seminary Biblical Counseling Program, *PsychoHeresy Awareness Letter*, Vol. 20, Nos. 4-6, 2012. References cited here can also be found at www.pamweb.org.

4   Elizabeth F. Loftus and Melvin J. Guyer. "Who Abused Jane Doe? The Hazards of the Single Case History," Part 1, *Skeptical Inquirer*, Vol. 26, No. 3, p. 24.

5   *Ibid.*, p. 25.

6   Paul E. Meehl. *Psychodiagnosis: Selected Papers*. Minneapolis: University of Minnesota Press, 1973, p. 227.

7   *Ibid.*

8   *Ibid.*, p. 228.

9   *Ibid.*, p. 229.

10   Lisa Mitchell, "Evoking the Inner Artist: How to Replace Pathology with Creativity," *Psychotherapy Networker*, Vol. 37, No. 5, p. 63; Dan Hughes, "Rewriting the Story: Entering the World of the Abused Child," *Psychotherapy Networker*, Vol. 38, No. 1, p. 57; Tana Dineen. *Manufacturing Victims.* Montreal: Robert Davies Multimedia Publishing Inc., 1996, 2000.

11   Mary Jo Barrett, "Outside the Box," *Psychotherapy Networker*, Vol. 38, No. 3, pp. 21-22.

12   Jacqueline Olds and Richard S. Schwartz. *The Lonely American.* Boston: Beacon Press, 2009, pp. 164-165.

13   *Ibid.*, p. 165.

14   *Ibid.*, p. 166.

15   Martin and Deidre Bobgan. *PsychoHeresy: The Psychological Seduction of Christianity* (Revised & Expanded). Santa Barbara, CA: EastGate Publishers, 2012.

16   Robert J. K. Law and Malcolm Bowden. *Breakdowns are good for you!* Bromley, UK: Sovereign Publications, 1999.

17   *Ibid.*, p. 2.

18   *Ibid.*, p. 3.

19   *Ibid.*, pp. 3-4.

20   Henry Wright. *A More Excellent Way.* Thomaston, GA: Pleasant Valley Publications, 2003, p. 140.

21   *Ibid.*, pp. 125-126.

22   Mary Sykes Wylie, "The State of Our Art," *Psychotherapy Networker*, Vol. 39, No. 2, p. 20.

23   David Murray, "Where is Biblical Counseling's Ken Ham?" http://headhearthand.org/blog/2014/02/07/where-is-biblical-counselings-ken-ham/.

24   Heath Lambert, "Who Is the Ken Ham of the Biblical Counseling Movement?" ACBC blog, 2/10/15, http://www.biblicalcounseling.com/blog/who-is-the-ken-ham-of-the-biblical-counseling-movement.

25   Michael J. Lambert. *Handbook of Psychotherapy and Behavior Change*, 5th ed. New York: John Wiley & Sons, Inc., 2004, p. 816.

26   *Psychotherapy Networker*, Vol. 31, No. 6, p. 2.

27   Kat McGowan, "The Power Couple," *Psychology Today*, November/December, 2004, p. 20.

28   "Therapeutic Alliance and Treatment Preference," *Harvard Mental Health Letter*, Vol. 24, No. 1, p. 7.

29   *Psychotherapy Networker*, Vol. 31, No. 6, p. 2.

30   John C. Norcross and Marvin R. Goldfield, eds. *Handbook of Psychotherapy Integration*, 2nd Ed. Oxford: Oxford University Press, 2005, p. 87

31   Arthur Shapiro interview by Martin Gross. *The Psychological Society.* New York: Random House, 1978, p. 230.

32   Hans Eysenck, "The Effectiveness of Psychotherapy: The Specter at the Feast," *The Behavioral and Brain Sciences,* June 1983, p. 290.

33 Robyn M. Dawes, *House of Cards: Psychology and Psychotherapy Built on Myth*. New York: The Free Press/Macmillan, Inc., 1994, p. 62.

34 *Ibid.*, p. 52

35 Larry E. Beutler, Paulo P. P. Machado, and Susan Allstetter Neufeldt, "Therapist Variables" in *Handbook of Psychotherapy and Behavior Change*, 4th Ed. Allen E. Bergin and Sol L. Garfield, eds. New York: John Wiley & Sons, Inc., 1994, p. 259.

36 Dawes, *op. cit.*, pp.101-102.

Chapter 3 "Organically Generated Difficulties"?

1   Jay E. Adams. *Competent to Counsel*. Grand Rapids, MI: Baker Book House, 1970, pp. 28-29.

2   Heath Lambert, "Can Jesus Heal Mental Illness?" Part 3, Biblical Counseling Coalition, May 16, 2014, http://biblical counselingcoalition.org.

3   "4 Controversial Mental Disorders," Paula Derrow, *Berkeley Wellness*, 9/10/2015, www.berkeleywellness.com.

4   "*DSM-5*: Psychiatrists' 'Bible' Finally Unveiled," *Huffington Post*, 05/16/2013, www.huffingtonpost.com.

5   E. Fuller Torrey, email 9/13/2014.

6   Erno Daniel. *Stealth Germs in Your Body*. New York: Union Square Press, 2008, p. 195.

7   *Ibid.*, pp. 196-197.

8   Thomas. R. Insel, "Atonement," www.psychiatrictimes.com.

9   *Psychology Today*, Vol. 35, No. 3, p. 17.

10 Mary Sykes Wylie and Richard Simon, "Discoveries from the Black Box," *Psychotherapy Networker*, Vol. 26, No. 5, p. 26.

11 Michael Chase, "The Matriculating Brain," *Psychology Today*, June 1973, p. 82.

12 Sidney Walker III. *A Dose of Sanity: Mind, Medicine, and Misdiagnosis*. New York: John Wiley & Sons, Inc., 1996, back cover.

13 Erich Kasten, "Ruled by the Body," *Scientific American Mind*, Vol. 22, No. 1, p. 53, 54.

14 Melinda Beck, "Confusing Medical Ailments With Mental Illness," *Wall Street Journal*, August 9, 2011, p. D-1.

15 "Idiopathic," www.en.widipedia.org/wiki/Idiopathic.

16 Robert M. Johnson. *A Logic Book*, 2nd Ed.. Belmont, CA: Wadsworth Publishing Company, 1992, p. 248.

17 *Blues Buster*, Vol. 2, No. 11, p. 1.

18 *Harvard Mental Health Letter*, Vol. 19, No. 7, p. 1.

19 K. Pajer et al., "Discovery of blood transcriptomic markers for depression in animal models and pilot validation in subjects with early-onset major depression," *Translational Psychiatry*, 4/17/2012, http://www.ncbi.nlm.nih.gov/pubmed/22832901; Marla Paul, "First Blood Test to Diagnose Depression in Adults," www.northwestern.

edu; "New Blood Test Can Identify Depression, *Mind, Mood & Memory*, December 2014, p. 2.

Chapter 4 Scriptures Misused, Abused, or Missed

1　William MacDonald. *Believer's Bible Commentary: Old and New Testaments*. A. Farstad, Ed. Nashville: Thomas Nelson, 1995, p. 838.

2　Matthew Henry. *Matthew Henry's Commentary on the Whole Bible: Complete and Unabridged in One Volume*. Peabody: Hendrickson Publishers, 1994, p. 995.

3　Mary Sykes Wylie, ""The CBT Path Out of Depression," *Psychotherapy Networker*, Vol. 38, No. 6, p 39.

4　Martin and Deidre Bobgan. *Stop Counseling! Start Ministering!* Santa Barbara, CA: EastGate Publishers, 2011.

5　Edmund Bolles. *Remembering and Forgetting*. New York: Walker and Company, 1988, p. 139

6　*Ibid.*, p. xi.

7　Nancy Andreasen. *The Broken Brain*. New York: Harper and Row, 1984, p. 90.

8　Carol Tavris, "The Freedom to Change." *Prime Time*, October, 1980, p. 28.

9　Christopher F. Chabris and Daniel J. Simons, "Why Our Memory Fails Us," *The New York Times*, 12/1/2014, www.nyt.com.

10　Bobgan, *Stop Counseling! Start Ministering! op.cit.*, Chapter 2.

11　Matthew Poole. *A Commentary on the Holy Bible*, Vol. II. Peabody, MA: Hendrickson Publishers, p. 549.

12　David Powlison, "Idols of the Heart and 'Vanity Fair,'" *The Journal of Biblical Counseling*, Winter 1995, pp. 35ff.

Chapter 5 Cross-Gender Counseling

1　Martin & Deidre Bobgan. *Stop Counseling! Start Ministering!* Santa Barbara, CA: EastGate Publishers, 2011, pp. 127-148.

2　Janet Raloff, "Chemicals from plastics show effects in boys," *Science News*, Vol. 176, No. 13, p. 10.

3　"The Neural Roots of Intelligence," *Scientific American Mind*, Vol. 20, No. 6, p. 30.

4　Larry Cahill, "His Brain, Her Brain," *Scientific American*, Vol. 292, No. 5, p. 40.

5　*Ibid.*, p. 41.

6　*Scientific American Mind*, Vol. 21, No. 2, cover.

7　Cristof Koch, "Regaining the Rainbow," *Scientific American Mind, ibid.*, p. 16.

8　Deborah Tannen, "He Said, She Said," *Scientific American Mind, ibid.*, p.56.

9　Louann Brizendine. *The Female Brain*. New York: Morgan Road Books, 2006, inside jacket cover.

10　*Santa Barbara News-Press*, Feb. 24, 2009, p. B5.

11   Jan Donges, "You Are What You Say," *Scientific American Mind*, Vol. 20, No. 4, p. 14.

12   *Ibid.*, p. 15.

13   "Gender Differences," http://en.wikipedia.org/wiki/Gender_differences.

14   Jeffrey A. Kottler. *On Being a Therapist*, 4th Ed. San Francisco, CA: Jossey-Bass, 2010, p. 144.

15   Alexandra G. Kaplan and Lorraine Jasinski in *Women and Psychotherapy: An Assessment of Research and Practice*. Annette M. Brodsky and Rachel T. Hare-Mustin. New York: The Guilford Press, 1980, p. 210.

16   Henri F. Ellenberger. *Discovery of the Unconscious: The History and Evolution of Dynamic Psychiatry*. New York: Basic Books/HarperCollins Publishers, 1970, p. 152.

17   *Webster's Encyclopedic Unabridged Dictionary of the English Language*. New York: Gramercy Books, 1996.

18   Garry Cooper, "Your Inner Therapist," *Psychotherapy Networker*, Vol. 34, No. 3, p. 11.

19   *Ibid.*

20   *Ibid.*

21   Ellenberger, *op. cit.*, p. 490.

22   http://en.wikipedia.org/wiki/Transference.

23   Jeffrey A. Kottler, *op. cit.*, p. 151.

24   Matthew Poole. *A Commentary on the Holy Bible*, Vol. III. Peabody, MA: Hendrickson Publishers, Inc., 2008, p. 28.

25   William MacDonald. *Bible Believer's Bible Commentary: New Testament*, Revised Edition. Nashville: Thomas Nelson Publishers, 1990, pp. 40-41.

26   Susan K. Golant, "Therapists Admit Sex Lure," *Los Angeles Times*, 6/24/1986, Part V, p. 1.

27   "Should Psychotherapist-Patient Sex Be a Crime?" *The Harvard Mental Health Letter*, Vol. 8, No. 9, p. 8.

28   "License to Harm," *The Seattle Times*, 4/23/2008.

29   Paul David Tripp. *Broken-Down House*. Wapwallopen, PA: Shepherd Press, 2009, p. 100.

30   *Ibid.*, p. 222.

31   Leslie Vernick. *How to Live Right When Your Life Goes Wrong* and *How to Act Right When Your Spouse Acts Wrong*. Colorado Springs: WaterBrook Press, 2003.

32   Holly Sweet, "Women Treating Men," *Psychotherapy Networker*, Vol. 34, No. 3, p. 34.

33   Concluded as a result of phone calls to or web site searches of all those organizations.

Case 1 "'Mariana' and Surviving Sexual Abuse"

1   John M. Grohol, "10 Common Reasons to Lie to Your therapist," *PsychCentral*, http://psychcentral.com.

2   Ryan Howes, "The Malleability of Memory," *Psychotherapy Networker,* Vol. 38, No. 6, p. 65.

3   Elizabeth Loftus interviewed in *ibid.*, p. 67.

4   See False Memory Syndrome Foundation, www.fmsfonline.org.

5   Jay Lebow. "War of the Worlds: Researchers and Practitioners Collide on EMDR and CISD," *Psychotherapy Networker*, Vol. 27, No. 5, p. 79.

6   Hans Eysenck, en.wikipedia.org.

7   Hans Eysenck,. cited by O. Hobart Mowrer. *The Crisis in Psychiatry and Religion.* Princeton, NJ: D. Van Nostrand Company, Inc. 1961, p. 133.

Case 2 "'Brian' and Obsessive Compulsive Disorder"

1   "Obsessive-Compulsive Disorder (OCD)," www.mayoclinic.org.

2   "What Causes OCD?" www.ocdeducationstation.org/ocd-facts/what-causes-ocd/.

3   "Obsessive-compulsive disorder," http://www.ncbi.nlm.nih.gov/pubmedhealth/PMH0001926/.

4   "Treating Obsessive-Compulsive Disorder," *Harvard Mental Health Letter*, Vol. 25, No. 9, p. 4.

5   Martin Seif and Sally Winston, "The Many Guises of OCD," *Psychotherapy Networker,* Vol. 35, No. 5, p. 17.

6   "OCD Diagnosis: OCD Criteria and Characteristics in DSM 5," http://www.healthyplace.com/ocd-related-disorders/ocd/ocd-diagnosis-ocd-criteria-and-characteristics-in-dsm-5/.

7   International OCD Foundation, www.iocdf.org.

8   "Treating Obsessive-Compulsive Disorder," op. cit.

Case 3 "'Sarah' and Postpartum Depression"

1   www.vocabulary.com/dictionary/documented.

2   Deborah A. Sichel, Lee S. Cohen, Laura M. Robertson, et al., "Prophylactic Estrogen in Recurrent Postpartum Affective Disorder." *Biological Psychiatry* , Vol. 38, No. 12, 1995, pp. 814-818.

3   Thomas Insel, "Spotlight on Postpartum Depression," NIMH, October 28, 2010, www.nimh.nih.gov.

4   Elizabeth Loftus interviewed in Ryan Howes, "The Malleability of Memory," *Psychotherapy Networker*, Vol. 38, No. 6, p. 67.

Case 6 "'Tony' and Bipolar Disorder"

1   "Bipolar disorder," www.nimh.nih.gov/health/topics/bipolar-disorder/index.shtml.

2   http://www.harvestbiblechapel.org.

3   Martin and Deidre Bobgan. Stop *Counseling! Start Ministering!* Santa Barbara, CA: EastGate Publishers, 2011, Chapter 7; Martin and Deidre Bobgan, "ABC, AACC, CCEF, NANC & 'Filthy Lucre,'" *PsychoHeresy Awareness Letter*, Vol. 17, No. 4, http://www.pamweb.org/abc_aacc.html.

4   www.twelvestones.org.

5   www.guidestar.org.

6   "How Sleep and Bipolar Disorder Interact," http://bipolar.about.com/cs/sleep/a/0002_mood_sleep.htm.

7   http://healthysleep.med.harvard.edu/need-sleep/whats-in-it-for-you/mood.

8   "Good night, sleep tight," *Mayo Clinic Health Letter* Special Report, 2014, p. 6.

9   "Sleep Deprivation," http://en.wikipedia.org/wiki/Sleep_deprivation.

10   See Chapter 4.

11   Martin and Deidre Bobgan, *Stop Counseling! Start Ministering! op. cit.*, pp. 72-79; "A Critical Review of The Master's Seminary Biblical Counseling Program," Part One, *PsychoHeresy Awareness Letter*, Vol. 20, No. 4.

Case 7 "'Jackie' and Dissociative Identity Disorder"

1   Two excellent examples of how those in the BCM get into the details of sex lives are found in *Stop Counseling! Start Ministering! op. cit.*, Chapter 3; Martin and Deidre Bobgan, "A Critical Review of The Master's College & Seminary Biblical Counseling Program, Part One, *PsychoHeresy Awareness Letter*, Vol. 20, No. 4.

2   "Status of DID Pt 1: Boysen & Van Bergen (2013) Paper: Is dissociative identity disorder (DID) an accepted and well-researched subject in the field of psychotpathology?" False Memory Syndrome Foundation News Alert, 6/42014, Part 1, www.fmsfonline.org.

3   "Dissociative identity disorder," http://en.wikipedia.org/wiki/Dissociative_identity_disorder.

Case 8 "'Jason' and Homosexuality"

1   "Argument from silence," en.wikipedia.org.

Case 9 "'Julie' and Addictions and Adultery"

1   Jay Adams. *Competent to Counsel*. Grand Rapids, MI: Baker Book House, 1970.

Chapter 7 "Concluding Reflections"

1   Martin and Deidre Bobgan. *Against "Biblical Counseling": For the Bible*. Santa Barbara, CA: EastGate Publishers, 1994, Chapter 6.

2   For example see Martin and Deidre Bobgan. *Stop Counseling! Start Ministering!* Santa Barbara, CA: EastGate Publishers, 2011, "Confronting and Commanding," pp. 78-79, in which Randy Patten orders a husband, in the presence of the man's wife, "No Bible, no TV!" thereby undermining the God-given role of the husband in the marriage.

3   Martin and Deidre Bobgan. *Person to Person Ministry*. Santa Barbara, CA: EastGate Publishers, 2009, pp. 42-52.; *Against "Biblical Counseling": For the Bible, op. cit.*, see particularly Chapter 3, pp.57-72.

4   Heath Lambert. *The Biblical Counseling Movement After Adams*. Wheaton, IL: Crossway, 2012 , p. 21.

5   William Kroger. "No Matter How You Slice It, It's Hypnosis" audio. Garden Grove, CA: Infomedix.

6   Martin and Deidre Bobgan. *Stop Counseling! Start Ministering!* Santa Barbara, CA: EastGate Publishers, 2011; *Person to Person Ministry, op. cit.*

7   We use the word *cure* throughout. Lambert prefers the term *heal*, as he has a series of blogs titled "Can Jesus Heal Mental Illness?"

8   We use the term mental *disorder(s)* throughout to mean mental-emotional-behavioral disorder(s).

Appendix Counselor, Counselee, Counseling

1   All biblical references in this section are from the Authorized King James translation.

2   *The Words of the Old Testament*, Vol. 1. R. Laird Harris et al., eds. Chicago: Moody, 1980, p. 390.

3   *Matthew Henry's Commentary in One Volume*. Grand Rapids: Regency Reference Library, Zondervan Publishing House, 1960, p. 91.

4   James Strong. *The Exhaustive Concordance of the Bible*. New York: Abington Press, 1894, 1967, "Hebrew and Caldee Dictionary," ref. 5971.

5   R. Laird Harris, Gleason L. Archer, Jr., Bruce Waltke. *Theological Word Book of the Old Testament*. Chicago: Moody Press, 1980, Vol. 1, p. 723.

6   James Strong. *The Exhaustive Concordance of the Bible. op. cit.*

7   Martin and Deidre Bobgan. *Against "Biblical Counseling": For the Bible*. Santa Barbara, CA: EastGate Publishers, 1994, pp. 57-72.

8   Jay E. Adams, "What is Biblical Counseling?" www.gateway-biblical-counseling. net/definition.html.

9   Jay E. Adams. *The Christian Counselor's New Testament*. Grand Rapids, MI: Baker Book House, 1977, 1980.

10   W. E. Vine. *The Expanded Vine's Expository Dictionary of New Testament Words*, John R. Kohlenberger III, ed. Minneapolis: Bethany House, 1984; Walter Bauer. *A Greek-English Lexicon of the New Testament and Other Early Christian Literature*, translated and adapted by William F. Arndt and F. Wilbur Gingrich, 2nd Ed., revised and augmented by F. Wilbur Gingrich and Frederick W. Danker. Chicago: The University of Chicago Press, 1957, 1979.

11   Jay E. Adams, "What is Biblical Counseling?" *op. cit.*

12   Martin and Deidre Bobgan. *Christ-Centered Ministry versus Problem-Centered Counseling*. Santa Barbara, CA: EastGate Publishers. 2004; *Person to Person Ministry*. Santa Barbara, CA: EastGate Publishers, 2009; *Stop Counseling! Start Ministering!* Santa Barbara, CA: EastGate Publishers, 2011 ; *Against "Biblical Counseling": For the Bible, op. cit.*

Martin and Deidre Bobgan's
published books are available
as free ebooks,
along with their free
articles and video links, at
www.pamweb.org/mainpage.html

9 780941 717243